The Collector's Encyclopedia of

Majolica

Mariann Katz–Marks

COLLECTOR BOOKS
A Division of Schroeder Publishing Company, Inc.

The current values in this book should be used only as a guide. They are not intended to set prices, which vary from one section of the country to another. Auction prices as well as dealer prices vary greatly and are affected by condition as well as demand. Neither the Author nor the Publisher assumes responsibility for any losses that might be incurred as a result of consulting this guide.

Searching For A Publisher?

We are always looking for knowledgeable people considered to be experts within their fields. If you feel that there is a real need for a book on your collectible subject and have a large comprehensive collection, contact Collector Books.

Additional copies of this book may be ordered from:

COLLECTOR BOOKS
P.O. Box 3009
Paducah, Kentucky 42002-3009

@ $19.95. Add $2.00 for postage and handling.

Copyright: Mariann Katz-Marks, 1992
Updated Values 1996

This book for any part thereof may not be reproduced without the written consent of the Author and the Publisher.

Printed by IMAGE GRAPHICS, INC., Paducah, Kentucky

═══ Dedication ═══

To my husband, Edward O.C. Marks, who proposed the original idea for this book and supported, encouraged and assisted me in every way possible during its preparation.

═══ Acknowledgments ═══

I especially thank my parents, Alice B. and Robert W. Katz, Sr., for their constant support and for their interest and encouragement in this undertaking. They provided me with the atmosphere in which creativity could flourish, and have been supportive in all my endeavors.

Thank you to our three daughters, Tamara, Irene, and Alice for their interest in this project and for being so understanding when Mommy was working on the book.

About the Author

Mariann Katz-Marks lives with her husband and their three children in rural Pennsylvania where she pursues a career selling English and American Majolica through an at-home mail order business and numerous antiques shows. Her fascination with this colorful Victorian ware began when she purchased a box lot of three Majolica plates at a country auction. Unsure of what they were, she located similar examples in a price guide and was lucky enough to have found two scarce Etruscan pieces! She holds a bachelor's degree in Psychology and completed graduate work in Sociology, Anthropology, and Clothing and Textiles. This background, as well as undergraduate training in art and photography, culminated in a true collector's appreciation for the form and beauty seen in nineteenth century Majolica and a desire to share her knowledge and photography with other collectors.

Table of Contents

Introduction

This new edition of *Collector's Encyclopedia of Majolica Pottery* incorporates all the photographs from my two previous books and includes many additional new pieces. I appreciate all the letters and comments on *Majolica Pottery*, Series One and Two. Many of you wrote to say how overjoyed you were to identify pieces in your collections and to discover the name of the potter or the year of manufacture. I hope this new book will add to your collecting pleasure and knowledge. I have enjoyed the project.

Often in my life Majolica collecting was shuffled to the back shelf while other events took precedence. Pieces I vowed never to part with are gone. My "complete" collection of Etruscan Bamboo is now half its original size. Suddenly I find an interesting piece and I am back to the pursuit of with renewed interest and dedication.

Collecting Majolica can be a delightful pleasure, a time consuming addiction, and a very interesting and educational look into history. I am always amazed as new patterns and types of Majolica are constantly encountered. In the years since I published my first book I have come to love it even more.

There is always a pleasant surprise in store for us down the road with the thrill and anticipation of the next discovery. I have spent many hours driving hundreds of miles across many states to attend an auction featuring Majolica. As I drive to an antique show, I find myself musing about what unknown wonder I will bring back home. Carry home your new acquisition, wash off one hundred years of grime, and find a place for it on the shelf to join the rest. Any dedicated collector will identify with these feelings! I hope you will experience some of the wonderful moments I have had in my collecting and selling career. I am happy to share them with you.

Collecting Majolica

Welcome to the wonderful world of Majolica where cauliflowers turn into teapots, fans become ice cream dishes, pickles are served from begonia leaves and sugar is spooned from a pineapple. At one time collectors of this colorful and whimsical Victorian pottery were few, but today there are many who faithfully attend antique shows, follow the antique shop trail, and sit out endless auctions in search of this brightly colored metallic glazed earthenware pottery produced by our ancestors.

There is an immense personal satisfaction to be enjoyed in the building of a collection no matter what its size or the extent of one's personal resources. Some dedicated collectors have flown around the world in search of Majolica and never miss an opportunity to pursue the hunt. Others search out additions to their collection at local flea markets and small antique shows. Some utilize mail order sources or attend local and distant auctions. No matter what the source or the funds expended in the search, the ultimate outcome is the same. You will experience the pleasure and inner satisfaction that comes from discovering gems of history and artistic beauty. The dedicated collector loves it all; the searching, bartering, carting it home, cleaning, labeling, cataloging, researching, and deciding on the proper display spot for each new acquisition.

The same Majolica that we collect today (related in name only to the fourteenth century Italian and Spanish ware) was loved avidly gathered by those who lived at the time of its production. I can envision our ancestors visiting shops and department stores to view the latest offerings of plates, platters, tea sets and pitchers from the world's Majolica potters.

Some collectors find that eventually they wish to specialize in one type of Majolica. For many, this is English Majolica. Almost all the well known manufacturers are represented including Wedgwood, Minton, George Jones, and Holdcroft. There are also many English pieces that cannot be readily attributed to these famous potters, but are very desirable in any collection. Generally, the English produced Majolica of extremely fine color and detail, adding significantly to their value.

Another collecting specialty is Etruscan Majolica made by the Pennsylvania firm of Griffin, Smith, and Hill. Pieces of Etruscan Majolica are highly sought after and the series contains some very desirable and beautiful specimens. There are collectors in the United States who have limited their collection to examples only by this manufacturer. Within that group are some who exclusively collect the very popular "Shell & Seaweed" pattern. Others try to find one example of each different pattern made by Griffin, Smith, and Hill, and still others try to obtain every pattern in all the sizes and colors that were produced. A collection of Majolica such as that can be the project of a lifetime.

Perhaps by far the greatest number of Majolica enthusiasts do not limit their collection in any way, trying to include attractive and desirable pieces by any potter from any country. These include items made in Germany, Austria, France, and Czechoslovakia, among others. Most of these are not truly of the Victorian period, but many collections are extended to include metallic glazed pottery of a naturalistic design no matter what the date of manufacture or country of origin. This would include the great body of interesting figural mouth-pouring pitchers that can form an outstanding collecting subset in themselves.

The best advice I can give on how to structure your collection is to acquire what appeals to you individually. This makes the most interesting and attractive display. Let your collection become a part of the joy of life and an expression of your sense of beauty.

The Potters

In the United States the largest producers of Majolica included Edwin Bennett of Baltimore, Maryland; James Carr, an Englishman transplanted to New York City, who formed the New York City Pottery Co.; James Scollay Taft who founded the Hampshire Pottery in Keene, New Hampshire; and George Morley of Wellsville and East Liverpool, Ohio. In addition there were the giants of the industry located in my home state, Griffin, Smith & Hill, of Phoenixville, Pennsylvania. David Francis Haynes, founded the Chesapeake Pottery Company, producer of the popular Clifton Decor line, in Maryland. Charles Reynolds of the New Milford Pottery Company, New Milford, Connecticut, and a group of potters in Trenton, New Jersey, populated an area that was to become known as the "Staffordshire of America" and included the Eureka Pottery Company.

On the other side of the Atlantic, in England, much Majolica was produced by Wedgwood, Minton, Copeland, Fielding, George Jones, Holdcroft, and the Victoria Pottery Company. We know this thanks to the beautifully marked specimens that delight today's collectors. The diamond-shaped English Registry mark found on the bottom of some pieces has revealed work by additional potters such as Shorter & Boulton, Stoke; Banks & Thorley, Hanley; Wardle & Co., Hanley; John Rose & Co., Coalport; and J. Bevington, Hanley, who produced an astounding tail feather pouring swan pitcher.

The French contributed many intricate figural pieces. They are known for an extraordinary array of collectible mouth-pouring pitchers and interesting Art Nouveau and Art Deco designs. Some of these pieces are later than the bulk of nineteenth century Majolica that interests most collectors but are often included in collections. They represent a continuation of the spirit and feeling of Victorian era Majolica and can stand on their own as representatives of their period. Do not, however, confuse these items with true nineteenth century Victorian Majolica made in the period of 1850–1900. At the same time the Austrians potted vast quantities of earthenware including a seemingly endless variety of figural tobacco humidors that are popular among collectors.

The experienced collector can generally distinguish American and English Majolica from that produced in other countries. Wares of countries other than the United States and England tend to be lighter in weight and do not usually display the typical motifs, construction, brush stroke markings, and glaze colors found on pieces of the Victorian period (1850–1900). The glaze colors are often stronger and of completely different tones than that appearing on American and English pieces.

American and English specimens are difficult to separate unless they are marked. Since many Englishmen moved to this country, bringing their molds and glaze formulas with them, it is easy to understand why the craftsmanship and motifs are so similar, if not identical. Many collectors limit themselves to pieces of American and English origin. In general, specimens from these countries are the most highly prized and collectible. In addition, some people like to include figural pieces and tableware from the Continental Majolica producing countries, such as France and Germany.

I hope you will enjoy looking through my photographs as much as I enjoyed producing them. Every piece of Majolica has its own place in the history of nineteenth century pottery and is a tribute to the innovative and creative potters who produced them.

Pricing

All prices are for items in generally good condition. Price ranges were taken from antique show sales, auction results, or published price lists. I tried to give a general range that would account for differences across the country. Please remember that prices tend to be higher in areas where Majolica is difficult to obtain and where many people are looking for it, such as in the Northeast. In areas where it is less well known, you may find greater bargains. It is still possible to find many pieces at less than the listed price with some diligent searching. Dealers not experienced in pricing and selling Majolica may place the same price on a rare piece as on a more common one.

Prices also tend to be higher near the East Coast and drop somewhat as one travels west. If you attend antique shows in large cities, the prices will be higher than in rural areas. An allowance has to be made when pricing in an area of the country where Majolica collecting has not yet caught on, or where generally lower values prevail. You may have purchased a piece identical with one in this book for much more or much less than the value I have listed. Remember, in the end there is no right or wrong price. In a free market such as exists in the antiques world, whatever one is willing to pay for a specific piece is the correct price.

This book is not meant to set prices or to tell you what you should pay. The true value of any item is what you feel it is worth to you. Often I have paid a premium for a new addition to my collection because it was worth it to me at the time. I may have owned the item once before and regretted selling it or I needed to fill a void in a particular part of my collection. The piece may be in exceptional condition, put away in a closet for over one hundred years and as beautiful today as when it was produced. I might pay more than the going rate if I seriously want the article. Most likely, a few years from the purchase date, I can look back and marvel at the "bargain" I got.

Small chips, age lines, and repairs do affect value somewhat, directly proportional to rarity. Defects devalue a common piece somewhat, while a skillfully done repair may not affect value at all for an exceptionally rare piece.

Majolica pricing is more accurately accomplished if the dealer or collector takes into account the desirable features of a particular piece. An attractive floral pitcher can be correctly priced at $95.00–125.00, but the same piece with the addition of a bird or a fan may be more properly priced at $200.00–250.00. It depends very much on the attractiveness of the item.

The addition of a potter's mark allowing one to identify the maker may place the value even higher. In general, marks in themselves do not add much for the typical collector if the piece itself does not display other virtues. More important than any mark is the level of craftsmanship, glaze color, and appealing motif. Keep this in mind if you have the tendency to collect by mark alone and are concerned with the value of your collection. The beautifully detailed and glazed unmarked piece is usually a good investment and should be chosen over a common marked example. If the marked piece is rare and unusual such as the Etruscan cow covered butter dish (see photo in Covered Pieces section) it has excellent investment potential though it is not too interestingly detailed or colored.

Condition

Most examples of nineteenth century Victorian Majolica did not survive their one hundred years of existence without some small reminder of the past. This shows up in age lines (hairline cracks) at the least and huge missing chunks, missing lids, or open cracks at the worst. The mint perfect piece of Majolica showing absolutely no sign of use or age is rare. Most collectors do not limit themselves to mint condition pieces only. To do so would severely limit the scope of their collection and many wonderful and important examples would go unrepresented. A collection assembled with condition as the prime factor might suffer blandness, consisting largely of common pieces and lacking many of those that lend depth and scope. A rare and unusual item that you find personally appealing should be accepted in spite of repair, but common pieces probably should be passed up by the serious collector if they contain major repair or damage.

Hairlines are hardly ever given serious consideration by the experienced Majolica collector. A good test to determine if an apparent hairline is actually a loose crack is to hold the piece to one's ear and wiggle both sides very gently. If the crack is loose, it will make a slight crunching sound. If a true hairline or age line, the piece will be silent!

Almost all Majolica has some evidence of its age and the glaze will have picked up small damages and discolorations. In addition, many pieces started life with some "in the kiln" imperfections, as it was not manufactured as carefully as fine porcelain. Majolica was made inexpensively enough to be used on a daily basis by the everyday household of the Victorian period.

Many pieces will be found in a stained condition, the result of years of use and the porous surface of this soft pottery. Although staining affects the appearance, it can usually be alleviated by a professional pottery cleaning process. One word of warning: never attempt to use chlorine bleach to clean Majolica as it may cause an eventual separation of the glaze from the body. This type of cleaning can destroy a beautiful piece.

When I get a new piece I give it a washing in a mild dishwashing detergent, using a plastic scrubber and a soft toothbrush to get off the accumulated grime. Always be gentle because the glaze will wear through with much abrasion. This type of scrubbing will be the last that it gets in my house, because I dust them with a damp cloth moistened with a "glass cleaner" solution that cuts any film that would otherwise build up through the years. It's really fun to get a bargain piece, all grimy from years of sitting in a forgotten cupboard, and see the gleam of the translucent glaze show itself again. It's amazing what a little gentle washing will do!

Baskets

BANKS AND THORLEY BAMBOO AND BASKETWEAVE BASKET. Part of the large series produced by this English company located in Hanley.

BASKETWEAVE BASKET WITH RIBBON TIED HANDLE. 10" l.

BIRD BASKET WITH RIBBON TIED HANDLE. 10" l.

BIRD IN FLIGHT EGG CUP BASKET. 9½" l. Six circular openings in the top are filled with little mottled egg cups, each with a lavender lining. One cup is missing here.

BIRD'S NEST BASKET. 9½" l.

CABBAGE LEAF AND DAISY BASKET. 12½" l. This basket has everything! Little yellow feet, and wonderful luggage strap handles.

CORSET LACED BASKET. 11½" l. The beautifully whimsical detail of corset lacing repeated around this basket sets it apart.

ORNATE HANDLED FOOTED FLORAL BASKET. 15¼" l. Exceptionally large with interesting details on the handle and feet.

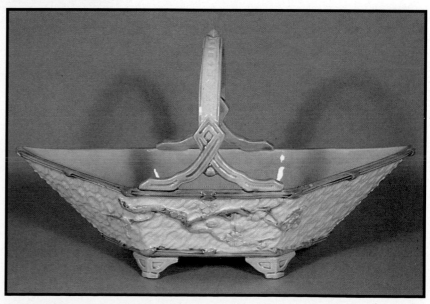

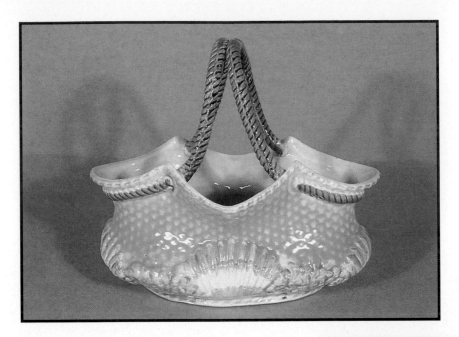

SHELL BASKET. 8½" L.

SIX SIDED FLORAL BASKET. Approx. 6" l.

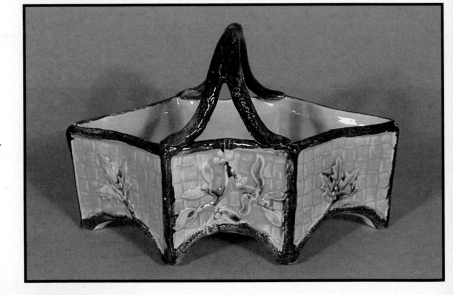

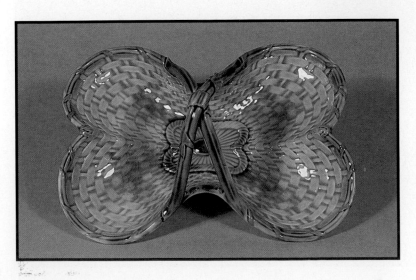

WEDGWOOD BASKET. 8" l.

CHESTNUT LEAF BOWL. 10" d. Is it or isn't it? Only the potter knows for sure. We cannot decide if this is a repaired bowl with the squirrel knocked off, or if the potter decided to produce a more economical version without the squirrel. The brown glaze you see here at the bottom of the photograph appears to be real glaze to me. I can almost always tell a repainting job because of the dullness of the repair when compared to original glaze, and the lack of translucency of the glaze. This has translucency and the shine but my husband feels it is rebuilt. The squirrel's feet would have to have been ground down and filled in along with a sophisticated job of re-glazing. Let us know what you think. Valued as a repaired piece.

CHESTNUT LEAF ON FOLDED NAPKIN BOWL. 9" d. 2¾" h. This bowl was produced from a George Jones mold but it is unsigned. Quite possibly a copy by one of Jones' contempories.

DUCK WASTE BOWL. 5½" d. Part of the tea set. Look for a sugar bowl and cream pitcher among others.

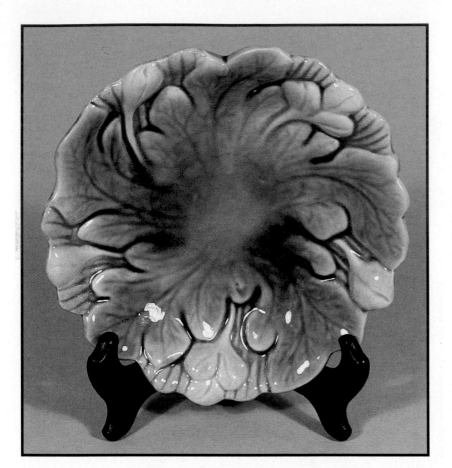

ETRUSCAN B4 LEAF DISH. 6" d. This little dish in attractive tones of green, brown and yellow is difficult to find. I have had just this one. It can be found in other color combinations.

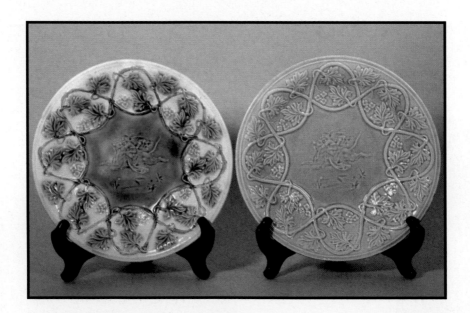

ETRUSCAN CLASSICAL SERIES BOWLS. 9¾" d. These are part of the large classical series produced by Griffin, Smith, and Hill depicting mythological scenes. Pieces of this series occur most often in the all over sepia coloring shown on the bowl at right. The colorful glaze treatment on the left is more scarce.

ETRUSCAN DAISY SAUCE DISH. 8¼" l. This came in two sizes and matches the Daisy Salad Comport.

ETRUSCAN GRAPE FRUIT DISH. 6½" d. This is the individual fruit dish that accompanies the oval grape fruit tray. This was done with background colors of white, as shown, pink and lavender, as was the grape fruit tray.

ETRUSCAN SHELL AND SEAWEED BOWLS. 8½" d., 5" d. The bowl on the left is the waste bowl to the shell and seaweed tea set.

ETRUSCAN SHELL FRUIT DISH. 5" d. This little dish belongs to the large family of Griffin, Smith, and Hill's shell and seaweed series.

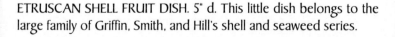

ETRUSCAN SHELL SALAD BOWL. 8¼" d. This style with seashells around the footed base is much more rare than the unfooted bowl. Circular Etruscan Majolica mark.

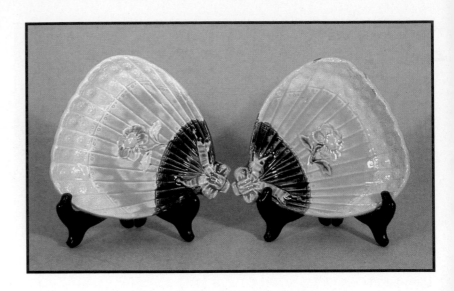

FAN AND BOW DESSERT DISHES. 6½" l.

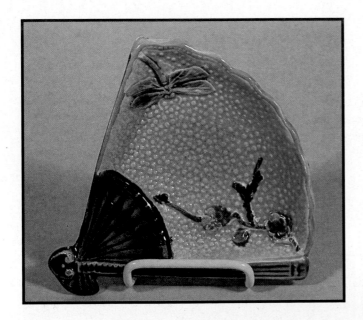

FAN SHAPED DISH. 6" d. A dragonfly swoops in on a prunus branch; these are fun to collect in sets. Watch for different background colors – it is attractive to mix the colors and use them for side dishes at the table.

GEORGE JONES BIRD ON EDGE OF BOWL. 7" d. A beautiful example of his way with birds; this little one is poised for flight on the edge of a beautiful turquoise dish supported on a thick twisted vine. Lovely holly leaves and berries complete the motif. A jewel!

GEORGE JONES DOGWOOD BOWL. 6" d. This bowl is part of Jones' dogwood series, a large group including cheese keepers and pitchers. A charming detail is the addition of twisted branch feet.

GEORGE JONES FLORAL STRAWBERRY SERVING DISH. 10" d. Two figural flowers form the cups for sugar.

GEORGE JONES MONUMENTAL SHELL BOWL ON PEDESTAL. 13" d. This piece is large and with unbelievable beauty and detail. The pinks are astounding and the detail on the base is so well done. The shell is supported above the base on a nest of white coral. Worthy of a central place in anyone's collection.

GEORGE JONES SMALL OVAL GRAPE PATTERN BOWL. 6" l. Unsigned but unmistakably Jones, part of his Bacchanalian series. The feet are gnarled grapevines.

GEORGE JONES TRIPLE LOBED LEAF RELISH SERVER. 12" l. Graceful white dogwood with a branch handle display George Jones' expertise using simple elements from nature. His pieces have a sophisticated grace almost unparalleled by any other potter except Minton.

HOLDCROFT POND LILY BOWL. 8" d. A nice little bowl which utilizes the pretty combination of browns and greens so typical of Victorian Majolica.

HOLDCROFT POND LILY BOWL. 11" d. Impressed J. Holdcroft. See mark No. 4.

HOLDCROFT SHELL ON PEDESTAL. 8" h. Very well done with nice nautical detailing on the pedestal. Signed Holdcroft.

HOLDCROFT SHELL-SHAPED BOWL. 9" d. Finely detailed bowl, held slightly aloft on shell-shaped feet. Signed Holdcroft.

HOLDCROFT TWIG FOOTED BOWL. 10½" l. Marked with the monogram JH in a circle. See mark No. 5.

LUGGAGE STRAP, CABBAGE LEAF AND FLORAL BOWL. 12" l. Identical in every respect to the basket pictured on page 11 except this one was designed without the handle for use as a bowl. Such a beautiful and unusual design. The Victorian potters were famous for their flights of whimsy.

MINTON RABBIT CENTERPIECE. 8" l. This piece is truly desirable from every aspect with these wonderful little bunnies crouching under the turquoise cabbage leaf surrounded by foliage. Whimsical pieces such as this are most desirable to many collectors.

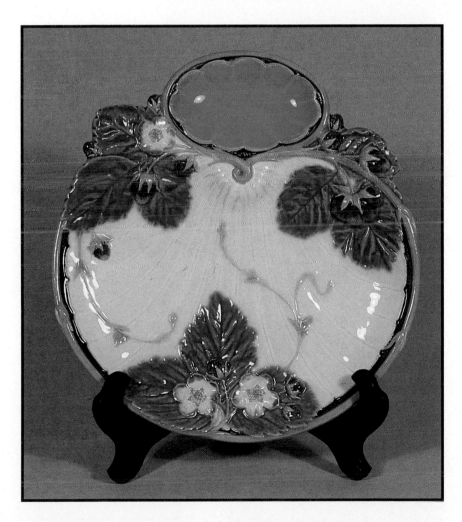

MINTON ROUND STRAWBERRY SERVING DISH. 9" d. Outstanding coloration marks this pretty strawberry dish. I believe these were intended as individual servers to be placed in front of every dinner guest at dessert time. The larger type with sugar and cream inserts were to be used in the center of the table.

MINTON SAILOR BOY SWEETMEAT DISH. 6" h. This is part of a large group of figural Minton dishes.

MINTON SIX-LOBED WATER LILY SERVING BOWL. 9" d. Minton displays ingenuity again with pond lilies in this attractive tiered relish server with small lily buds protruding from under the three larger leaves. One central figural flower serves as a handle.

MORNING GLORY AND PICKET FENCE DISH. 9" d. A deep plate or dish with an attractive fence pattern.

PICKET FENCE BOWL. 9" d. The interior has an unusual turquoise, brown, and white mottling instead of the more traditional lavender or turquoise.

PICKET FENCE AND MORNING GLORY DEEP DISH. 7" d. A picket fence pattern surrounds the mottled center.

ROUND ALBINO DISH. 9½" d. Unusual albino coloration on a serrated edged dish with open handle.

SHORTER & BOULTON BIRD AND FAN SAUCE DISHES. 5" d. Shorter and Boulton, Stoke, England, registered this design on March 17, 1881. They all bear the English Registry mark. These are a good example of difference in quality of glaze. While the bowl on the left has perfectly acceptable coloring, the one on the right is much more intense and desirable.

SQUIRREL NUT SERVING BOWL. 10" d. This is probably an American version of the George Jones piece. The detail is not as fine as the English, but many American Majolica collectors find in this rustic beauty the essence of what makes Majolica so appealing. Large green chestnut leaf dominates the center of the bowl. The figural squirrel is holding a nut!

STRAWBERRY BLOSSOM BOWL. Approx. 5" d. A beautiful cobalt background sets off this unmarked piece.

TURQUOISE SCALLOPED TOP FLORAL BOWL. 9" d. 4" h.

TWIG HANDLED FOOTED BOWL. 9". This was also made with serpent handles and without handles. The color of the flowers will vary.

UNUSUAL SIX-SIDED BOWL. 15" l. Turquoise basketweave and pink prunus blossoms decorate the body of this unusual six-sided bowl. Lovely rich lavender lining.

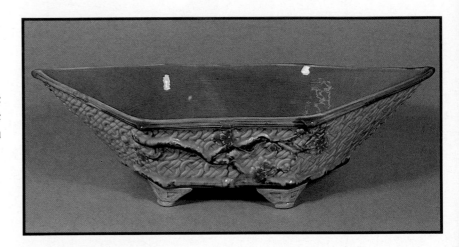

WARDLE BIRD AND FAN FOOTED VEGETABLE BOWL. 10" l. Manufactured by Wardle & Co., Hanley, England. One of a large series of pieces produced by this company, they all bear the English Registry mark.

WARDLE SUNFLOWER BOWL. 10½" l. This design was registered to Wardle & Co., Hanley, England, on July 19, 1882, patent #383641. Also in a platter.

WEDGWOOD BIRD PERCHING ON EDGE OF DISH. 7" d. The delicate beauty of this is hard to believe. The little bird is poised over a group of white pond lilies floating on a cobalt blue dish. A rare piece which I have seen only once.

WEDGWOOD CREAM BOAT, OPEN SUGAR BOWL AND STRAWBERRY SERVING DISHES. Cream boat, 3" h. Open sugar bowl, 3" h. Strawberry serving dishes, 6¾" d.

WEDGWOOD FAN AND PRUNUS SMALL DISH. 6½" d. This abstract fan pattern compliments the larger rendition of the design to be found on the bird and fan pieces. Marked Wedgwood.

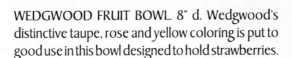

WEDGWOOD FRUIT BOWL. 8" d. Wedgwood's distinctive taupe, rose and yellow coloring is put to good use in this bowl designed to hold strawberries.

WEDGWOOD OVAL BASKETWEAVE AND GRAPE LEAF BOWL. 12" d. This pretty piece has such delicate handles in the shape of gnarled grapevines. Caution is advised when purchasing this — I have had them with broken handles which have been re-glued. It is a very hard piece to find in perfect condition. Still very beautiful and worthwhile even with imperfections! Look for this also with a white background instead of the cobalt.

WEDGWOOD OVAL CENTERPIECE BOWL WITH LEAFY GARLAND. 15" l. This bowl incorporates a beautiful cobalt blue base with yellow wicker basket work around the top. The graceful drape of the garland is accented with pink ribbons. Signed Wedgwood.

WEDGWOOD ROUND CENTERPIECE BOWL. 12" d. Beautiful example of Wedgwood's attention to detail, the garland is encrusted with flowers and wrapped with ribbon. Yellow wicker detailing on the top.

WEDGWOOD SHELL DISH. 6" d.

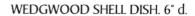

BROWN, WESTHEAD, MOORE & CO. COMPOTE.
8½" d. 7" h. The name is impressed on the underside
of one of the twig feet. Marked English pieces such as
this are rare and desirable. Rare mark.

COBALT BELLFLOWER COMPOTE. 9½" d. 5" h. Also
in a plate.

ETRUSCAN DAISY SALAD COMPORT. 9" d. 5" h. These were made with a white background and a cobalt background.

ETRUSCAN MORNING GLORY COMPOTE. 8" d. This hard-to-find compote does not usually turn up in very good condition. I have seen them signed and unsigned, and with a very rare, bright red background. This example in mint condition.

FAN CAKESTAND. 9" d. I have had this pattern in a plate but had never seen it in a low cakestand!

ETRUSCAN SHELL & SEAWEED CAKESTAND. 9" d. A rare piece, and one hard to find in good condition. I have never seen one without repair, which of course is perfectly acceptable in rare pieces. These must have been used very frequently in the Victorian household.

FIELDING SNAIL SHELL HIGH CAKESTAND. 9½" d. 5¼" h. English Registry mark and FIELDING impressed. See mark No. 6. Part of a series of fishnet covered pieces displaying a variety of seashells. Includes pitchers, teapot, sugar and cream pitcher, and a low cakestand.

GEORGE JONES BACCHANAL COMPOTE. 6" l. This diminutive compote could grace the serving table at your next wine party. Two cherubs hold the small bowl aloft, each lying on a goatskin bulging with wine.

GRAPE LEAF COMPOTE. 8½" d. 4½" h. This is a copy of a Wedgwood pattern.

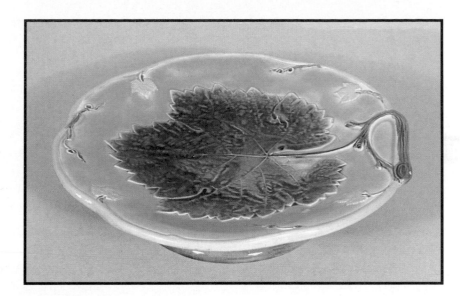

LEAF ON PLATE LOW CAKESTAND. 9" d.

MINTONS CUPID COMPOTE. 6½" h. Graceful and classic interpretation of the cupid theme. They support the oval lobed compote on their wings with two kissing doves in the central area adding an unusual touch. Signed MINTONS with the number 930 and the year mark for 1875.

NEW ENGLAND ASTOR CAKESTAND. 9" d. 2" h. Many pieces were produced in this pattern which is attributed to James Scollay Taft of the Hampshire Pottery, Keene, New Hampshire. Look for a large vegetable bowl, platter, plates, teapot, mug, butter pats, tea set, spooner, high cakestand and a spice tray with handle.

PINEAPPLE COMPOTE. 9" d. 4¾" h.
One of the major Majolica motifs. A
large variety of ware was produced in
the pineapple pattern.

SHELL AND SEAWEED LOW CAKESTAND. 8½" d. 2¼" h. Part of a large
series of pieces which included a cake plate, cup and saucer, bowl, and a
high cakestand among others.

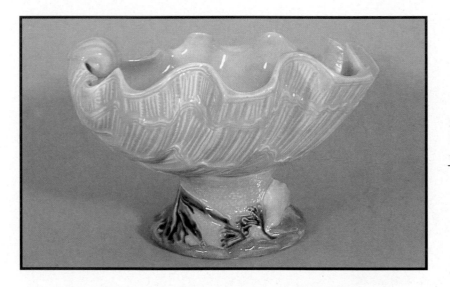

SHELL COMPOTE. 9" d. 6" h. This large handsome salad
bowl is attributed to Morley. They were produced in
yellow and turquoise.

Above: WILD ROSE AND ROPE COMPOTE. 9¾" d. 6"h. Also
in a turquoise background.

Left: WORCESTER DOLPHIN COMPOTE. 9" d. 7" h. Possibly
the piece copied by Griffin, Smith and Hill when they produced
their L2 dolphin comport, this is almost identical except for the
base. The Worcester mark is impressed underneath inside the
pedestal. See mark No. 8.

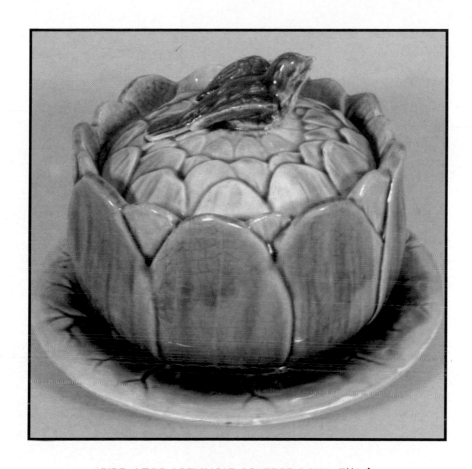

BIRD ATOP ARTICHOKE COVERED BOWL. 7¼" d.

BANKS AND THORLEY BASKETWEAVE AND BAM-
BOO COVERED BUTTER DISH. 8" d.

COBALT AND FLORAL BUTTER DISH. 7½" d. The cobalt blue adds extra value.

ETRUSCAN BAMBOO COVERED BUTTER DISH. 6½" d.

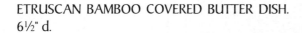

ETRUSCAN COW BUTTER DISH. 7¾" d. This is one of the rarest Etruscan pieces. Also in yellow and green mottling.

ETRUSCAN SHELL & SEAWEED BUTTER DISH. 4" h. This one is rare and desirable and may take a while to find to complete your shell and seaweed collection. I have been fortunate enough to have had two. It also comes in another variation with a different arrangement of shells on the cover.

RASPBERRY BUTTER DISH. 7" d. Rustic tree bark background with a mottled green and brown glaze.

SHELL, SEAWEED, AND WAVES BUTTER DISH. 7" d.

SUNFLOWER WITH FLY BUTTER DISH. 6¾" d.

WILD ROSE BUTTER DISH WITH ROPE TRIM. 6½" d. This pattern was produced in a variety of pieces including platters, tea sets, plates, and compotes. The background colors vary and include cobalt, blue-grey and turquoise.

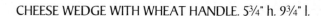
CHEESE WEDGE WITH WHEAT HANDLE. 5¾" h. 9¾" l.

COW FINIAL CHEESE KEEPER. 11½" h. 12¾" d. This is truly a monumental piece. Unsigned, but the workmanship and coloring allow an attribution to the pottery of George Jones, Stoke on Trent.

ETRUSCAN SWAN CHEESE KEEPER. 7½" h. with 8" d. base. Extremely rare! This example is in perfect condition. This pattern is referred to as "Lily covered cheese, No. N5 in the Griffin, Smith & Hill Catalogue of Majolica" reprinted in 1960. This is one of two covered cheese dish patterns made by this Pennsylvania company.

GEORGE JONES DAISY AND FENCE CHEESE KEEPER. 11" h. For those who love George Jones Majolica (I never met a collector who did not like the work of this pottery), this stupendous cheese keeper will be the centerpiece of the collection. The cobalt blue background is particularly effective. Everything about this large and beautiful piece is ideal.

GEORGE JONES DOGWOOD CHEESE KEEPER. 10" h. Slightly smaller and more squat than most cheese keepers, this belongs to George Jones' large series of dogwood pieces. The design also occurs in pitchers, larger cheese keepers, plates, etc.

GEORGE JONES DOGWOOD AND WOVEN FENCE CHEESE KEEPER. 10½" h. 11½" d. Impressed with the English Registry mark and the JG monogram. See mark No. 3. Also in a tea set with tray, a small pitcher and a smaller version of this keeper without the fence. The impressive skills of one of England's finest craftsmen is presented in full form here! Superb!

HERON CHEESE KEEPER. 11" h. One of the nicest cheese keepers I have ever seen. It was not made in the "Wedgwood" school of pottery but by one of the less well known English potters whose name at this time is still a mystery. For them, this was a major piece and much attention to detail can be seen in the lovely cattails, and in the lavish coloring of the bird. Look at the gracefulness of this large heron with his catch for the day clasped in his beak! He is standing in a bed of pond lilies outlined with bamboo. This piece is representative of what is so appealing about Majolica.

HOLDCROFT OAK LEAF CHEESE KEEPER. 5" h. This one is much smaller than usual, and the motif is kept very simple. Still, it is appealing and pretty with a nice figural handle.

HOLDCROFT POND LILY CHEESE KEEPER. 9" h. Especially beautiful coloration, the white lilies seem to float on the green lily leaves. The handle is one beautiful lily bud. I have seen it in two sizes. This is the smaller one.

HOLLY CHEESE KEEPER. 10½" h. 10½" d.

ROPE AND FERN CHEESE KEEPER LID. 8" h. Such a pretty lid with its lavender background stands on its own without the base. I always pick up these odd lids and bases when I can; I have actually put them together years after the purchase of individual components.

WEDGWOOD CHEESE KEEPER. 10" h. Yellow floral and green leaf cheese keeper with a brown basketweave base. Any cheese keeper is hard to find but those by Wedgwood are particularly scarce.

ETRUSCAN SHELL CIGAR BOX. One of the rarest pieces in Griffin, Smith and Hill's shell and seaweed series.

GEORGE JONES QUAIL AND RABBIT GAME DISH. 12" l. I know I will not be able to do justice to this piece with mere words. The picture speaks for itself. I must say that this is a personal favorite and a good example for students of Majolica; it demonstrates all the elements that go into making a very valuable addition to one's collection.

MINTON GAME DISH. 12" l. This Minton game dish is a very desirable piece, has a large sculptured hare and mallard duck on the lid. The base is a realistic brown basketweave with graceful oak leaves.

WEDGWOOD RABBIT GAME DISH. 7" l. A nice example of Wedgwood's use of the classic Majolica colors of green and brown – the rabbit crouches atop the dish. Around the base are representations of various game animals surrounded by garlands of greenery. The Wedgwood pottery was particularly fond of various types of garlands. This is the small one. It came also in a larger size.

GEORGE JONES MATCH BOX WITH STRIKER ON BOTTOM. 4" l. This diminutive piece has the George Jones signature seal on the underside of the lid and the underside of the base is ridged to be used as a striker. Most unusual.

BASKET OF FISH SARDINE BOX. 8½" l. Unusual open handles on the attached underplate. A prize example, probably George Jones.

COBALT AND LEAFY GARLAND SARDINE BOX. 9½" l. Nice workmanship and color. Attached underplate.

COBALT AND SEAWEED SARDINE BOX. 7½" l. Attached underplate.

CONCH SHELL AND BASKETWEAVE SARDINE BOX. 8½" l. A nice design employing a shell finial instead of the more typical fish. The underplate is attached.

ETRUSCAN SARDINE BOX. 6" l. Try to add this to your Etruscan collection if you can find it. I have also seen it with a different color background. The design is almost identical to the George Jones sardine box, although here the more rustic modeling and the Etruscan coloration is unmistakable.

FLORAL AND FENCE SARDINE BOX. 7" l. Most sardine boxes are decorated with various types of fish, so this nice floral rendition is refreshingly different. Bowls can also be found in this pattern. The turquoise area represents a picket fence.

GEORGE JONES SARDINE BOX. 8½" l. 7¾" w. Both the box and the separate underplate are signed. These pieces display all the beauty of color and quality of workmanship one expects from a George Jones piece. Also in a turquoise background. The box and the underplate will be found both with a variety of marks and unmarked. See marks No. 1, 2, and 3.

GEORGE JONES DUCK FINIAL SARDINE BOX. 5¾" l. This large beaked fellow has had some restoration to his head and the original beak was probably much smaller. Unusual to find a sardine box with other than a fish finial. Rare.

HOLDCROFT POND LILY SARDINE BOX. 8" l. This is one of the more unusual boxes. The detail of the little fish swimming on the side adds interest as do the pretty white lily buds on each corner. The fish are particularly realistic. This is the only sardine box by Holdcroft I have been able to photograph, although other designs must exist.

MINTON SARDINE BOX. 9" l. Impressed Minton. Attached underplate. Minton pieces are among the finest.

PINEAPPLE SARDINE BOX. 9½" l. Attached underplate.

POINTED LEAVES SARDINE BOX. 9" d. Attached underplate.

POND LILY AND BAMBOO SARDINE BOX. 9" l. Impressed V.P.C. with two swords forming a triangle.

ROPE EDGE SARDINE BOX. 8" l. This sardine box is attractive in the more rustic style, as opposed to the finely detailed pieces of the major English potters, eg. Jones, Minton, and Wedgwood. Most Majolica falls into the rustic category.

SHELL FINIAL SARDINE BOX. 7" l. I had never seen this one before. The coloring is very pleasant and the big shell finial adds value.

SWAN FINIAL SARDINE BOX WITH DOLPHIN FEET. 5¾" l. A beautiful swan preening his feathers and gliding through pond lily leaves. The four dolphin feet and the cobalt ground add to an already outstanding piece. An example of excellence in design.

"UNDER THE SEA" SCENE SARDINE BOX. 6½" d. Unusual form around the base.

WEDGWOOD BOAT SARDINE BOX. 9" l. I have also had this with a white background. It has the words "Sardinia" impressed on the side. Outstanding about this is its figural boat shape with fishnet draping down each side.

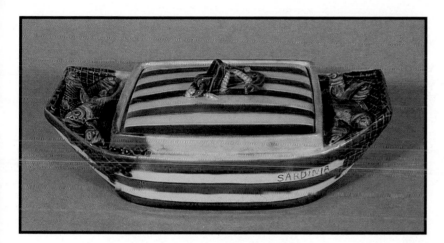

WEDGWOOD BOAT SARDINE BOX. 8" l. Here is the same sardine in the white striped version.

YELLOW BASKETWEAVE SARDINE BOX. 5½" l.

ETRUSCAN ALBINO OAK SOAP BOX. 6" l. I feel so fortunate to have had this in my possession for a short time and to have photographed it. I know this has to be among the rarest of Majolica. The oak soap box is a great rarity in the Etruscan series, but this one is even more unusual because it is done in the albino coloration. Among albino pieces, this is also a rarity because it utilizes three shades of luster, a pale yellow, a deeper saffron, and a beautiful shade of pink. There is a liner inside. Signed.

CHILD ON CLOTHES TRUNK TOBACCO BOX. 6" l. A boy lies atop a large clothing trunk eating a huge slice of pink watermelon. Although the boy is American, the box was made in Austria and is unusual. Austrian tobacco boxes usually portray figural animals. Desirable for collectors of tobacco boxes, Majolica, and figurals.

AVALON "SUNNY BANK" PUSH-UP TOBACCO HUMIDOR. 9" h. "Sunny Bank" is the name of the tobacco produced by Spaulding & Merrick in Chicago. A nice example of Majolica produced as advertising by the Chesapeake Pottery Company. Printed Avalon Faience mark.

BISON HEAD COVERED JAR. 5" h. Incised in freehand script, "Austria."

FRENCH FAIENCE BEAK-POURING PARROT PITCHER. 11" h.

FRENCH FAIENCE BEAK-POURING ROOSTER PITCHER. 12" h. This is not a typical Majolica glaze.

MORLEY FISH BOUQUET HOLDER. 6¾" h. Marked GEORGE MORLEY'S MAJOLICA. EAST LIVERPOOL, O. Morley also made a large fish but the detailing and workmanship is not as good as the small "bouquet holder."

MORLEY OWL PITCHER. 8¼" h. Marked MORLEY & CO. MAJOLICA, WELLSVILLE, O. The glazing is done in typical Majolica style on white ironstone instead of the usual earthenware. These pieces are particularly desirable because they are figural, marked, and American.

PAIR OF MOUTH-POURING PUG PITCHERS. 7½" h. and 10½" h. These wonderful looking fellows have hand-carved teeth and the larger of the two has rake-like scratches in his clay to simulate fur. Most unusual and thought to be American.

PARROT PITCHER. 11¼" h. This stately bird is remarkable for his size and the good detail and coloring of his feathers. Made in a variety of sizes, this was probably the largest. Many smaller examples do not display the high relief of the feathers and good coloring of this specimen.

PELICAN PITCHER. 9" h. Unusual handle on a very desirable figural piece.

PIG WAITER MOUTH POURING PITCHER. 10¾". One of a number of interesting French pieces by a producer who marked his wares "Frie Onnang," and sometimes included crown and shield.

TOBACCO HUMIDORS. BULLDOG WITH MUG OF BEER, 7¾" h. "ALICE" BULLDOG, 4" h., hat impressed "Alice." FROG STRUMMING A MANDO-LIN, 6¾" h.

WING HANDLED DUCK BEAK-POURING PITCHER. 11" h. Marked "Made in Portugal." 20th century. A type of brightly colored faience pottery resembling Majolica and included in collections of figural pieces.

COBALT MUG WITH SUNFLOWER. 3½" h. CLIFTON DECOR MUG. 3½" h. Printed "Clifton Decor" mark. See mark No. II. ETRUSCAN PINEAPPLE MUG. 3½" h. Marked only with the decorators black stenciled number, these mugs are always attributed to Griffin, Smith and Hill but are never marked with the GSH monogram.

COBALT WITH TRAILING IVY MUG. 4" h.

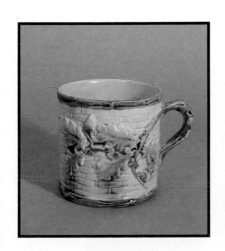

ETRUSCAN ACORN MUG. 3½" h.

ETRUSCAN FOOTED LILY MUG. 4" h. These are never signed.

FLORAL MUG. 4" H.

HOLDCROFT LILY MUG. 3½" h. Impressed J. Holdcroft.

FROG AND FERN ON BAMBOO MUG. 4½" h. Two figural frogs surprise the unwary drinker when he nears the bottom!

PANSY SHAVING MUG. 3½" h. Quite rare, the lavender interior has a divider with a section for the shaving lather. Straight line impressed mark, probably Fielding.

PICKET FENCE AND FLORAL MUG. 3¾".

RASPBERRY MUG. 3½" h. Red raspberries and blossoms curl around a yellow ridged background. Turquoise banding top and bottom and a pretty pink interior. Mugs are relatively hard to find and make a nice sub-collecting specialty.

ALL TAN HAWTHORNE PITCHER. 5¼" h. These are always unsigned but are considered to be Etruscan. They also occur in all-over green and all-over cobalt. The reason for the unconventional decoration and the unsigned base remains a mystery. They could have been a special "budget" order for some retail outlet, an experiment with a less costly method of operation by Griffin, Smith, and Hill themselves, or pieces given free of charge to the pottery workers for their own use.

ADAMS AND BROMLEY LILY PITCHER. 8" h. This design was registered to Adams and Bromley of Hanley, England, on August 21, 1882, patent #385129. English Registry mark.

ARRAY OF CREAM PITCHERS AND A SPOONER. Right to Left: OWL AND FAN SPOONER, 4½" h. FIGURAL FISH CREAM PITCHER, 3¼" h. DUCK CREAM PITCHER, 3¾" h. FISH HANDLED ANCHOR CREAM PITCHER. 4½" h.

BANANA LEAF PITCHER. 6¼" h. Brown banana leaves with turquoise embossed floral patter at top. Lavender lining.

BAMBOO AND BOW PEWTER TOP PITCHER. 6" h.

BANKS AND THORLEY BASKETWEAVE AND BAMBOO PITCHER. 7½" h.

BANKS AND THORLEY PEWTER TOP SYRUP PITCHER. 7½" h. English Registry mark.

BARK SQUARES WITH KNURLED BASE PITCHER. 7½" h. Also made in a tea set.

BASKETWEAVE AND FENCE FLORAL PITCHER. 6" h.

BASKETWEAVE AND FLORAL PITCHER. 6" h. Red flowers and green leaves on a yellow basketweave ground. Brown rope handle.

BENNETTS SUNFLOWER SYRUP PITCHER. 7¾" h. Marked BENNETT'S JAN. 28, 1873, PATENT. This is the year the design was registered with the patent office and not necessarily the year of manufacture.

BENT TREE TRUNK PITCHER. 7" h.

BEVINGTON SWAN ON PITCHER. 8½" h. This design was registered to the firm of J. Bevington, Hanley, England on November 21, 1881, patent #373575. Remarkable because of its unusual form, the swan pours through its tail feathers with the neck forming the handle. English Registry mark.

BIRD AND BASKETWEAVE PITCHER. 8½" h.

BIRD AND IRIS FOOTED CREAM PITCHER. 4" h. Compare this to the Etruscan Bird and Iris pattern – nearly identical except this example is footed.

BIRD AND POND LILY PITCHER. 8" h.

BIRDS AND NEST PITCHER. 7" h. This birds nest has the eggs already hatched! Also look for a version with unhatched eggs.

BIRDS FEEDING YOUNG IN NEST. Approx. 6" h. English Registry mark. Two birds are feeding a nest full of young.

BIRDS NEST PITCHER. 9¼". This is typical of the work of an unknown potter (probably American) who made a variety of pieces with these "tree knurls" protruding around the base.

BLACKBERRY PITCHER. Approx. 7½".

BLACKBERRY PITCHER. 8" h. This is the king of the blackberry pieces with its good workmanship, vibrant coloring, and large size.

BLACKBERRY AND PICKET FENCE PITCHER. 7" h.

BLACKBERRY FENCE PITCHER. 7¼" h.

BOW AND FLORAL SYRUP PITCHER. 8¼" h.

BUTTERFLY AND BAMBOO CREAM PITCHER. 3" h. This little cream pitcher utilizes the butterfly theme to full effect, surrounding it with a frame of bamboo.

BROWNFIELD IVY PITCHER. Approx. 8" h. Brown and green mottling with the Brownfield pottery mark on the bottom.

BUTTERFLY AND FLORAL CREAM PITCHER. 3½" h.

BUTTERFLY LIP FLORAL PITCHER. 7" h. The design of this is so similar to the Etruscan butterfly lip pitcher. This is either a forerunner or copy by an unknown potter.

"CAN'T YOU TALK?" PITCHER. 8" h. This lovely example of a child and a dog is distinctive not only for depicting a human being on Victorian Majolica, but also for the distinctive legend underneath, "Can't You Talk?"

CHICKENS WITH WHEAT SHEAF PITCHER. 7" h. This wonderful piece portrays two chickens going around a sheaf of wheat – a good example of how amusing and whimsical Majolica motifs can be. Probably English.

CLIFTON DECOR FRUIT PATTERN PITCHER. 6½" h. Clifton decor mark. See mark No. 11.

COBALT AND FLORAL PITCHER. 5½" h.

COBALT FLORAL PITCHER. 8" h. This combination of colors is very desirable – cobalt, pinks, greens and yellows.

COBALT PEWTER TOPPED PITCHER. 4½" h.

COBALT, FLORAL, AND BASKETWEAVE PITCHER. 6½" h. The coloring and exceptionally deep embossing of the flowers, as well as the shape make this one really special! Lavender lining.

COPELAND EGYPTIAN LOTUS PITCHERS. 6½" h. and 8¼" h. Clearly a masterpiece of design and workmanship, these pitchers rank among the highest achievements for English potters of the period. Impressed COPELAND along with the English Registry mark, the design was registered on July 2, 1877, patent #311523. The larger is impressed 6.Gill and the smaller is impressed 3.Gill above the Registry mark.

DOGWOOD AND LILAC BARREL STAVE PITCHER. 8"
h. This is an outstanding piece of work. The colors are
really clear, with a yellow rope around the top and a very
clean shiny glaze.

DOGWOOD ON BARK OVAL PITCHER. 8" h. This pretty oval shaped pitcher
was unsigned but the colors are in imitation of Wedgwood. You will notice
the distinctive taupe color on the handle and branches.

DOGWOOD ON MOTTLED GROUND PITCHER. 5½" h.
Pink dogwood with green leaves overlay a mottled green
and brown background. Particularly lovely coloring.

DRAGON HANDLED FLORAL PITCHER. 8¼" h. Unusual winged dragon figural handle. Also in a larger size with a yellow background.

DUCK IN FRAME FLORAL PITCHER. 7½" h. This is one of my favorites. A duck swims on a turquoise pond surrounded with an embossed rectangular frame. A nautical rope loops over the bottom of the frame and connects it to the identical frame on the other side. Rope also adorns the handle.

ENGLISH COTTAGE PITCHER. 7" h.
Quite unusual and well done.

Above: ENGLISH ROSE PITCHER. 6" h. Cobalt coloring adds to the
beauty of this English pitcher.

Left: ETRUSCAN ALBINO CORAL SYRUP PITCHER. 7" h. Another
rare and unusual Etruscan piece. The albino decoration is quite well
done here. Usually it is not as colorful.

ETRUSCAN ALBINO SHELL PITCHER. 5¾" h. The base bears the circular Etruscan Majolica mark.

ETRUSCAN ALBINO SUNFLOWER PITCHER. Approx. 6" h. This rare Etruscan albino pitcher is unmarked as are almost all the albino examples.

ETRUSCAN BAMBOO SYRUP PITCHER. 8" h. These have recently gone at wildly divergent prices, both lower and higher than those listed here.

ETRUSCAN BASEBALL AND SOCCER PLAYERS JUG IN FULL COLOR. 7¾" h. This Griffin, Smith and Hill jug is among the most rare of all the Etruscan series. Modeled in the manner of a Wedgwood jug, it displays the particularly American sport of baseball – the Wedgwood jug portrays cricket players. This example is signed. Extremely rare in multi-color with the GSH mark.

ETRUSCAN CORAL CREAM PITCHER. 3½" h. Griffin, Smith and Hill made these little pitchers in a variety of sizes. They are all hard to find.

ETRUSCAN CORAL SYRUP PITCHER. 6¼" h. The small size sets this apart from other Etruscan syrup pitchers.

ETRUSCAN CORN CREAM PITCHER. 4" h. These can be marked with the catalog number only, E5, or with the decorator's black stenciled identification number only.

ETRUSCAN CORN PITCHER. 6" h. Another Etruscan rarity made by a famous American potter of the nineteenth century, Griffin, Smith and Hill

ETRUSCAN FERN PITCHER. 8¼" h. Potted in a variety of sizes.

ETRUSCAN MONOTONE BASEBALL PITCHERS. 7¾" h. The baseball pitcher was also done in all-over monochrome and are unsigned as is usually the case. Rare.

ETRUSCAN RUSTIC PITCHER. 8¼" h. Griffin, Smith and Hill potted these in five sizes.

ETRUSCAN SHELL AND SEAWEED PITCHERS. Left to Right: 6¾" h. 4¾" h. 5¾" h. 3½" h. Considered to be one of the most beautiful patterns ever made by Griffin, Smith and Hill, these pieces are avidly sought by most collectors. Shell patterns and marine themes were one of the most popular Majolica motifs. Look for other shell motifs produced by Wedgwood, Fielding, and James Carr of the New York City Pottery Co., among others.

ETRUSCAN SUNFLOWER PITCHER. 6½" h. The sunflower pitcher was made in a variety of sizes with three background colors. The cobalt is pictured here. They also came in white and pink.

ETRUSCAN SUNFLOWER SYRUP PITCHER. 8" h. These lovely pieces were produced with cobalt background as shown here and also with a white and a pink ground.

ETRUSCAN WILD ROSE PITCHER. 8" h. The wild rose pitcher with its butterfly lip was produced in a variety of sizes, the smallest being a tiny cream pitcher.

FAN AND SCROLL WITH INSECT PITCHERS. 4½" h. and 5½" h. English Registry mark. This interesting pattern always combines a fan with a small insect and a scroll bearing an impressed clipper ship. Other pieces in this pattern with the impressed maker's mark allow an attribution to S. Fielding & Co., Stoke, England.

FAN, BUTTERFLY AND CRICKET PITCHER. 8¾" h.

FERN ON BARK PEWTER TOP PITCHER. 7" h.

FIELDING BUTTERFLY AND BAMBOO PITCHER. 6" h. This is unmarked but the glaze and black pen marks on the underside all say "Fielding." The colors are particularly vivid and it has a pretty lavender lining.

FIELDING FIGURAL SHELL PITCHER. 8" h. The body of this graceful piece represents a figural shell, with ocean waves splashing at the base, quite a beautiful form. Pitchers such as this with a figural quality are particularly desirable.

FIELDING SHELL AND FISHNET PITCHER. 7" h. Also in a teapot, cream pitcher, lidded sugar bowl, and a waste bowl. English Registry mark.

FIGURAL CREAM PITCHERS. Approx. 4½". This spaniel and owl are collectible as figurals, as cream pitchers, and as Majolica.

FIGURAL OWL PITCHER. 9½" h. This is a very nice example of an owl. Note the open figural flower on top of the leafy handle.

FISH PITCHER. 7½" h. English Registry mark. Possibly Shorter & Boulton.

FISH ON WAVES PITCHER. 8¼". Beautiful coloring and lusterous glaze. There is another pitcher with the identical form but a slightly different handle and one similar to this, but with a different top and bearing the English Registry mark. This is unmarked. A splendid example of a fish pitcher.

FLORAL PITCHER. 7" h.

FLORAL PITCHER. 5" h. The pitcher has a yellow sunflower and green leaves on one side and small pink flowers on the other. The background is brown bamboo.

FLORAL PITCHER. 5" h. This one is the same as the preceding floral pitcher but this time the ground is in turquoise and I am showing the opposite side with the small pink floral motif.

FLORAL PITCHER. 5¾" h. Red flowers on a brown ground with yellow embossed designs at top and bottom.

FLORAL AND ANCHOR PITCHER. 8¼" h. Unusual anchor and chain pattern around the top and pale pink flowers with green leaves in the center. Brown basketweave bottom.

FLORAL AND CORN CREAM PITCHER. 4½" h. Tiny ears of embossed corn surround the top with trails of reddish flower hanging from a brown rope band. Majolica cream pitchers can form an interesting and attractive collection in themselves!

FLORAL AND BASKETWEAVE PITCHER. 6" h. Pale, pale pink flowers and green leaves top a brown basketweave bulbous base.

FLORAL AND DRAPERY PITCHER. 6" h. Turquoise draperies trimmed with yellow ruffles and tied with a bow set off the pretty reddish flowers. This has the Rd mark and the design was probably registered between 1889 and 1890. However, it also includes the impression "Made in England" which indicates this particular piece was made during the twentieth century.

FLORAL TURQUOISE BANDED
PITCHER. 8¼" h.

GEORGE JONES DOGWOOD PITCHER AND CHEESE KEEPER LID. Pitcher,
5½" h.; lid only, 8" d. The pitcher design was registered to George Jones, Stoke,
England, on February 25, 1873, patent #270700. It has the English Registry mark
only and no George Jones signature. The lid to the small cheese keeper is in
the same pattern. Jones also produced a tea service and tray with the dogwood
design. Refer to the "Covered Pieces" chapter to view this pattern in all its
magnificence as a large cheese keeper.

GEORGE JONES IRIS AND LILY
PITCHER. 6¾" h. Perfectly exquisite, it
is not difficult to see why George Jones
Majolica is considered among the best.
GJ monogram is in a circle.

GEORGE JONES MONKEY HANDLED
PITCHER. 7" h. English Registry mark.
Also in a tea set on tray.

GEORGE JONES UNDERWATER PITCHER. 8" h. The small band at the top represents the sky with gulls soaring overhead. Underneath are a variety of fish, crabs and underwater plant life! Quite a display and a very attractive piece.

GREEN LEAF SYRUP PITCHER. 4" h. Attractive earthtones and a nice shape give this little one value.

GREEN LEAF AND FLORAL PITCHER. 7" h. Probably Holdcroft.

HOLDCROFT DOGWOOD SYRUP PITCHER. 4" h. This is a tiny version of the larger Holdcroft dogwood pitchers.

HOLDCROFT DOGWOOD PITCHER. 9" h. The coloring on this one is very nice. These also came with a white background.

HOLDCROFT PEWTER TOP LILY PITCHER. 4¾" h. Impressed J. Holdcroft.

HOLDCROFT POND LILY PITCHER. 7½" h. This cylindrical, oval pitcher has all the fine detail usually found in pieces from this major potter. The green pond lily leaves overlap and there is the added bonus of a figural pond lily bud on the top of the handle. This is the type of detail that adds value.

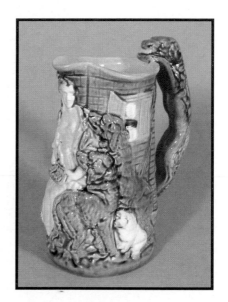

HOUND HANDLED WOMAN FEED-
ING DOGS PITCHER. 6" h. Very rare
hound handle. Also unusual for Majolica of this period to portray a woman.

HONEY BEAR FIGURAL PITCHER. 9" h. This amusing bear belongs
to the family of mouth-pouring pitchers. The handle forms a spoon.

HUMMINGBIRD PITCHER. 6¼" h. This fluffy hummingbird is coming in
for a landing on the red prunus blossom. The background is stippled
off-white.

HUMMINGBIRD PITCHER. 9" h. This one has such a nice shape from the bulbous turquoise basketweave base to the scalloped edge around the top. Notice the detail on the brown handle.

IVY ON TREE BARK PITCHER. 8" h. Simply done interpretation with the classic browns and greens. English.

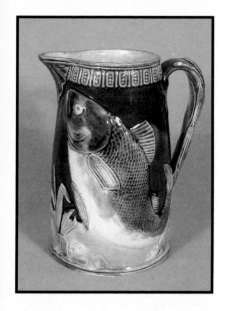

JRL FISH PITCHER. 7" h. Impressed JRL on the footrim. Possibly J. Roth, London, who registered designs c. 1882.

LEAF SPOUT AND ROSE AND BASKETWEAVE PITCHER. 9¼" h. The immense size distinguishes this one. Made in various smaller sizes, this is probably the largest.

LEAF SPOUT FLORAL AND BARK PITCHER. 7" h. Careful workmanship and lustrous glazes combine with an unusual leaf treatment.

LITTLE GIRL AND DOG PITCHER. 8" h. Highly unusual in that it features a little girl. Designers of this period followed an unwritten rule and generally did not include people in their designs.

MAPLE LEAF PEWTER TOP SYRUP PITCHER. 7" h.

MERMAID PITCHER. Approx. 9½" h. Unusual figural handle and high quality relief work and glazing. Attributed to J. Holdcroft, Longton, England.

MINTON PITCHER. 8" h. This piece is distinguished by its intensity of coloring and simplicity of design. Most Minton pieces have more elaborate decoration, however, this is very appealing nonetheless.

MINTON COURT JESTER JUG. 13" h. This splendid and imposing piece used the court jester as a finial. The body displays various figures along with grape motifs; most certainly a jug for serving wine.

MONKEY FIGURAL PITCHER. 9" h. I just love these pitchers. I have had them in 8", 7" and 5" sizes as well, all with a lavender lining. Scarce!

MORLEY SYRUP PITCHER. 8¼" h. Also on white ironstone as are the Morley owl and fish bouquet holder. The base is marked MORLEY & CO. WELLSVILLE, O.

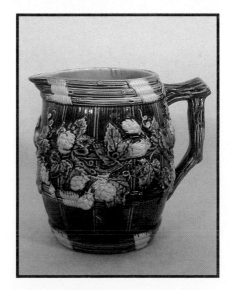

OAK BARREL AND AVOCADO PITCHER. 5½" h. Unmarked but possibly George Jones. Heavy green and brown mottled base.

OWL AND FAN TRIANGULAR PITCHER. 7½" h. Beautiful in every aspect with a fan spout, bamboo handle, and bamboo leaves on the back. These were made in a variety of sizes. There is at least one size larger. Also with a grey background.

PEAS IN POD PEWTER TOP PITCHER. 5½" h. Also in a larger version without the pewter top.

PEWTER TOPPED CORN PITCHER. 9½" h. The English Registry mark, pewter top, rich color of the glazes, gracefullness of form, and the stately size combine to make this a beautiful example of England's rendition of the corn pattern. Many corn pattern pieces were also produced in America.

PEWTER TOPPED PINEAPPLE SYRUP PITCHER. 5¼".

PINEAPPLE PITCHER. 8" h.

POND LEAF PITCHER. 7" h. Overlapping green pond lily leaves cover the body of this unusual one. Yellow leaves surround the top.

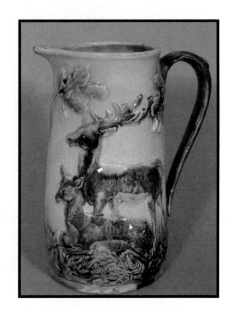

REINDEER PITCHER. 7½".

RED RASPBERRY PITCHER. 5" h. Red raspberries and flowers are embossed on an off-white fence pattern.

ROBIN ON A BRANCH PEWTER TOP PITCHER. 4½" h. Remarkable for its tiny size. Also in a larger version without the pewter top.

ROBIN ON BRANCH PITCHER. 7½" h. The same unknown potter also produced a very similar design but with a different style of bird. Coloration varies.

RUNNING ELEPHANT PITCHER. 7½" h.

RUSTIC BLACKBERRY PITCHER WITH TREE KNURL BASE. 5½" h.

SAMUEL LEAR PITCHER. 9" h. The English Registry mark tells us that this impressive piece was registered on December 14, 1882. The number is 391409. Note the oriental influence in the fan designs shaping the upper rim.

SAMUEL LEAR SUNFLOWER AND CLASSICAL URN CREAM PITCHER. 3½" h. Part of a large series including platters, plates, cake stands, and a mustache cup and saucer. English Registry mark.

SAMUEL LEAR SUNFLOWER AND CLASSICAL URN SYRUP PITCHER. 8" h. Here is the pretty Samuel Lear sunflower design done in a tin-topped pitcher.

SHARKSKIN AND FLORAL BOW PITCHER. 8¼" h.

SHEAVES OF WHEAT PITCHER. 6". A solid green ground sets off plump yellow and brown sheaves of wheat.

SHELL AND SEAWEED PITCHER. 7½" h. English Registry mark. Notice how this has much sharper detail than the previous unmarked pitcher of the same design. In my personal collection, it is one of my favorite pieces. I purchased it from Charles Rebert, author of *American Majolica.*

SHELL AND SEAWEED PITCHER. 7½" h. This pitcher is almost identical to the one above but there is no marking and the details are not as sharply impressed. A wonderfully executed design!

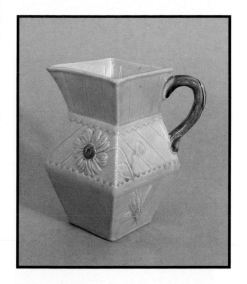

SQUARE TOPPED FLORAL PITCHER. 6" h.

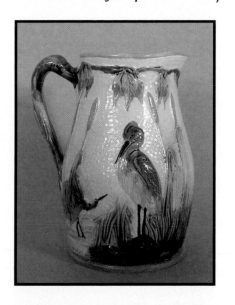

STORK IN A MARSH WITH EEL HANDLE PITCHER. 9½" h. This is a splendid example of a bird pitcher with colorful cattails, a smaller bird and a figural handle which could be an eel.

STORK IN A MARSH WITH OVERHEAD FISH. 9". This wonderful pitcher has such an interesting motif with a bamboo base and a large stork standing in the marsh complete with cattails. What appears to be a bird flying overhead, upon closer inspection, is actually a fish. I have no explanation other than a flight of fancy on the part of the artist.

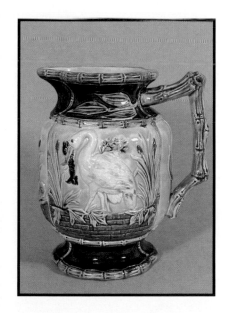

STORK WITH FISH IN MOUTH PITCHER. 8¼" h. A very desirable piece with beautiful high relief and very careful decoration. The artistry of design is quite evident here. The pattern was also produced by George Jones.

SWALLOW ON BRANCH PITCHER. 8¾" h. A speckled base has a very large pond lily blossom with leaves. The top is unusual because of the rectangular shape and beautiful scroll designs. Another of my personal favorites!

SYRUP PITCHERS. 4¾" to 6" h. Many of the larger pitchers were also made in these diminutive sizes with pewter lids.

TREE TRUNK AND FLORAL PITCHER. 7" h. This closely copies a Wedgwood design.

TURQUOISE AND BASKETWEAVE THREE LEAF PITCHER. 8" h. This came in graduated sizes, including a small syrup pitcher with a pewter lid.

WARDLE BIRD AND FAN PITCHER. 7¼" h. Also in a larger size and cream pitcher size. English Registry mark.

WARDLE FERN AND BAMBOO PITCHER. 7½" h. Part of the large fern and bamboo series produced by this English company. English Registry mark.

WATER LILY AND DRAGONFLY PITCHER. 7½" h. A lily bud atop the handle and the dragonfly make this an unusual piece.

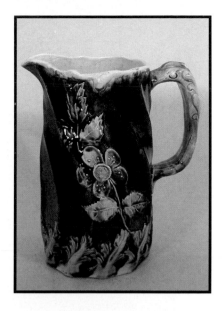

WAVY BACKGROUND FLORAL PITCHER. 8" h. Unusual for the curved background and the grey embossed handle.

WEDGWOOD BIRD AND FAN PITCHER. 10" h. Wedgwood's beautiful color and detail combined with the enormous size make this an outstanding piece. Probably made for display only, when full, it is too heavy to handle. Impressed "Wedgwood."

WHITE BARK AND GREEN LEAF PITCHER. 5½" h. A large green leaf and ferns with pink tinges are laid over a white bark ground.

WICKER SYRUP PITCHER (missing pewter lid). 6¼" h. Attributed to George Jones. Lavender base.

WILD ROSE PITCHER WITH BUTTERFLY LIP. 7" h. This is an unmarked copy of the Etruscan wild rose version. Very vivid coloring with striking lavender interior. Brown branch handle.

WILD ROSE ON TREE BARK PITCHER. 9½" h. A beautiful example of this fairly common pattern. In addition to the turquoise pictured here, it came in additional background colors of white and brown. This piece is particularly large.

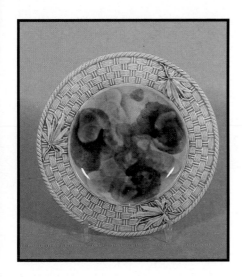

BANKS AND THORLEY BAMBOO AND BASKETWEAVE PLATE. 7¾" d. Also a tall coffee pot, tea kettle, teacup with butterfly handle, basket, and pitchers and syrup pitchers among others. Unmarked.

BANKS AND THORLEY CAKE PLATE. 10" d.

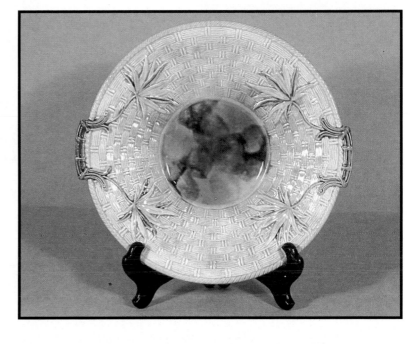

BANKS AND THORLEY FERN AND BOW PLATE. 8" d. English Registry mark. This concern located in Hanley, registered the design on April 10, 1883 with patent #396648.

BIRD IN FLIGHT TURQUOISE PLATE. 8½" d. Attributed to J. Holdcroft.

BLACKBERRY AND BASKETWEAVE PLATE. 10½" d. Unusual for its large size and turquoise background. Most commonly found in a smaller size with a white background.

BOW ON BASKETWEAVE PLATE. 6" d. This plate is part of a larger set which included a large platter and a tea set.

ETRUSCAN ALBINO SHELL AND SEAWEED PLATE. Approx. 8" d. No mark as usual with the albino pieces. This is a very nice example of the shimmery kind of gold glaze Griffin, Smith and Hill used.

ETRUSCAN APPLE AND STRAWBERRY PLATE. 9" d. This particular plate was one of the first pieces of Majolica I ever bought and it remains a favorite to this day. Look also for background colors of pink and blue.

ETRUSCAN BEGONIA LEAF TRAY. 9" l. Also produced in an 8" version. Coloration varies. These were originally intended as pickle dishes.

ETRUSCAN CAULIFLOWER PLATE. 9" d. These were also made in a 6" and a 7" size.

ETRUSCAN CLASSICAL SERIES PLATE. 8" d. Here is one of a whole series of classical pieces made by Griffin, Smith and Hill. This plate has the "corn" border. I once had a cup and saucer to match with an all-over corn pattern.

ETRUSCAN CLASSICAL SERIES PLATE. 9" h. Marked with the GSH monogram. See mark No. 10.

ETRUSCAN DOG PLATE. 9" d. A very rare example of a plate that falls into the Classical Series. A setter-type dog sits at attention in the center in an all-over green glazed field. The pinky-beige surrounding border is embossed with floral garlands draped through rings. This plate is part of my personal Etruscan collection and is very dear to my heart. The only one I have ever seen!

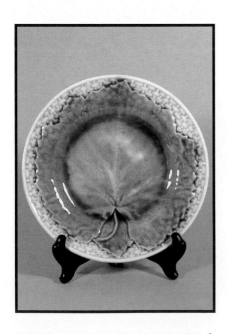

ETRUSCAN LEAF ON PLATE. 7¾" d. Also in an 8¾" d.

ETRUSCAN MAPLE LEAVES PLATE. 9" d. Pictured here in the pink and white backgrounds, it was probably also produced in blue.

ETRUSCAN SHELL AND SEAWEED PLATE. 9" d. The 9" version of this Etruscan plate is much more rare than the 6" or the 8" sizes.

ETRUSCAN STRAWBERRY PLATE. 9" d. This was also produced with a white background. The blue is uncommon.

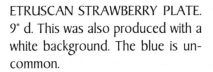

FERN AND FLORAL PLATE. 8" d.

FIELDING FAN PLATE. 8³/₄" d. Impressed FIELDING. These were produced both signed and unsigned.

FIELDING FAN OYSTER PLATE. 9" d. Here is an unusual one for either Majolica or oyster plate collectors. It is signed Fielding, and has a nice combination of colors and design. Each indentation for an oyster is an oriental fan.

FISH OYSTER PLATE. 10" d. Also in another version without the large fish.

FLORAL AND THREE LEAF PLATE. 9" d.

FLORAL BORDERED PLATE. 9" d. Probably George Jones.

GEORGE JONES OYSTER PLATES. 8¾" d. Impressed with the George Jones monogram.

GEORGE JONES OYSTER PLATE WITH FIGURAL SHELL. 10" d. The remarkable thing about this is the center shell which is raised.

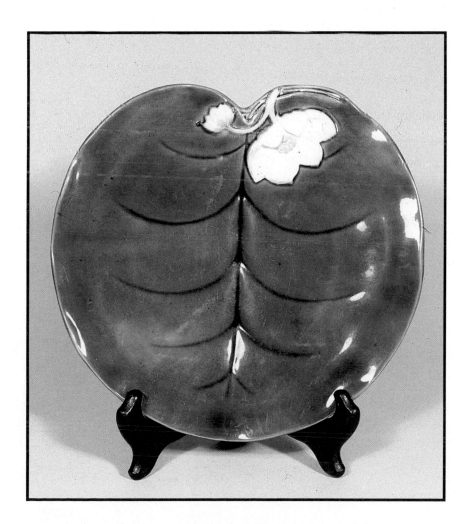

GEORGE JONES WATER LILY PLATE. 8" d. These are fun to collect in sets. If you seach diligently you may be able to find the matching cakestand.

GERANIUM FLORAL PLATE. 9" d. Pink and white geranium blossoms and green leaves on a brown background. I kept this plate for many years before parting with it. Always a favorite, I have only had this one.

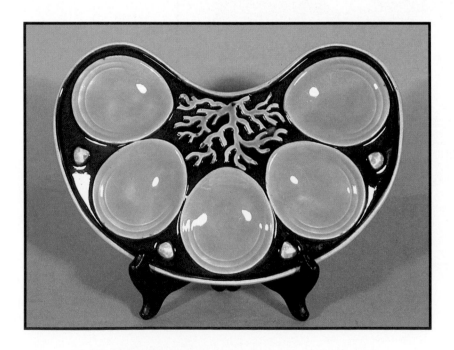

HALF-MOON SEAWEED OYSTER PLATE. Approx. 8" d.

HOLDCROFT BASKETWEAVE AND FLORAL PLATE. 9" d. Impressed JH monogram. See mark No. 5.

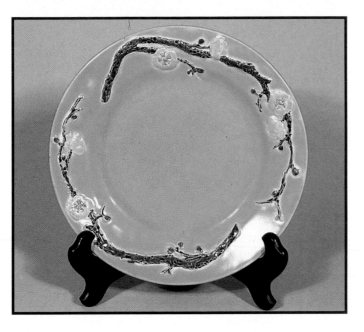

HOLDCROFT DOGWOOD PLATE. 8" d.

HOLDCROFT FISH PLATE. 8½" d. Impressed J. Holdcroft.

HOLDCROFT FISH AND DAISY PLATE. 9" d. This nice fish also appears on plates with a turquoise background.

HOLDCROFT WATER LILY PLATE. 8" d. The coloration here is elegantly simple and the graceful lines quite effective. Despite its simple theme, this was one of my favorite plates for a long time.

LOBE-EDGED MORNING GLORY PLATE. 9" d.

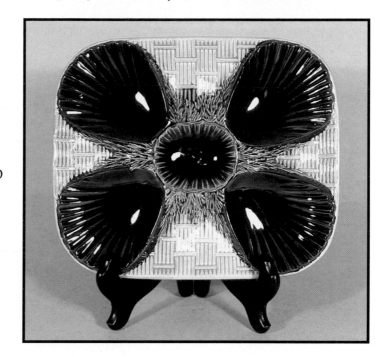

MINTON BASKETWEAVE AND SEAWEED
OYSTER PLATE. 9" l. Impressed Minton.

MINTON OYSTER PLATE. 10" d. A deep cobalt
mottling marks this handsome piece.

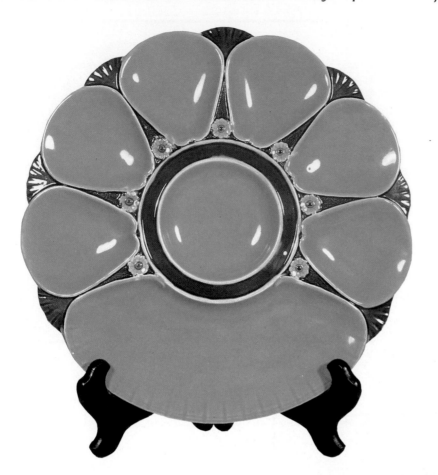

MINTON OYSTER PLATE. 10" d. Here is the same plate as the one on the previous page in a different coloration with turquoise.

MINTON WATER LILY PLATE. 9" d. This restrained interpretation of the classic water lily theme is so effective. This set consisted of 12 plates and one huge platter.

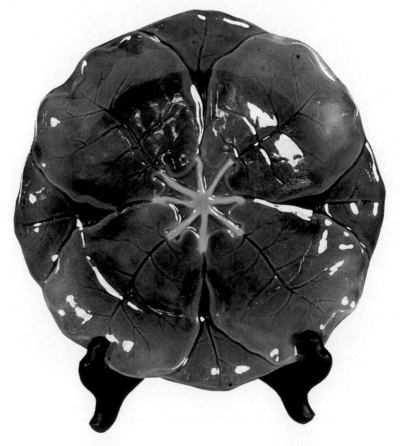

MORLEY NAPKIN PLATE. 8" h. Marked MORLEY & CO. MAJOLLICA, WELLSVILLE, O. White ironstone instead of the earthenware body.

MOTTLED CENTER PLATES. Right to left: Etruscan Bamboo plate. 8" d. Cobalt border and floral plate. 9½" d. This may be an underplate missing the lid. Etruscan Rose plate. 7" d. Etruscan underplate to the Lily cheese keeper. 11½" d. Also produced as a bread tray. In that form it lacks the ridge to hold the top in place which is present on this piece.

MULTI-COLOR SHELL OYSTER PLATE. Approx. 10" d.

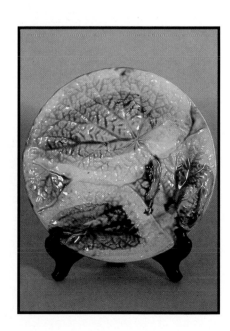

OVERLAPPING BEGONIA LEAVES PLATE. 8¾" d.

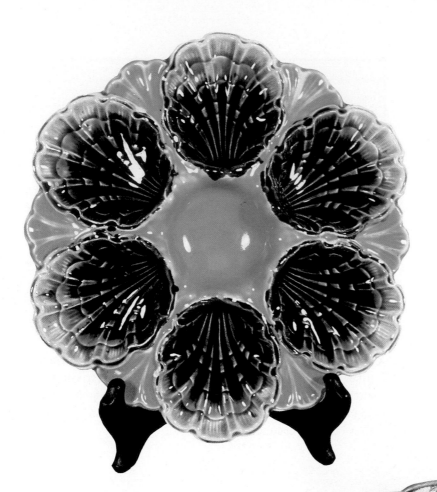

OYSTER PLATE. 9" d.

OYSTER PLATE. 9" d.

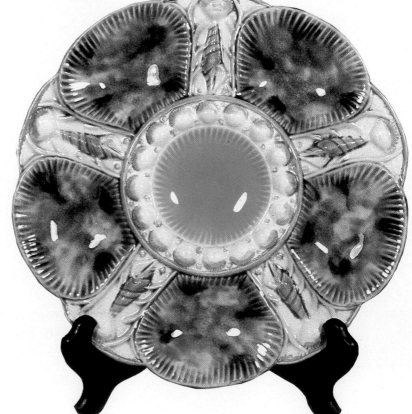

OYSTER PLATE. Approx. 9" d. This is the same pattern as the famous Minton oyster plate, but this example is unmarked. It is very common to find unmarked examples of the designs of Wedgwood, Minton and George Jones that were copied by other English and American potters.

PARROT, BUTTERFLY AND BAMBOO PLATE. 9" d. This fellow was registered in England in 1884 and bears the impressed registry mark Rd No. 3119.

PINEAPPLE PLATE. 9¼" d.

PINEAPPLE PLATE. 9" d.

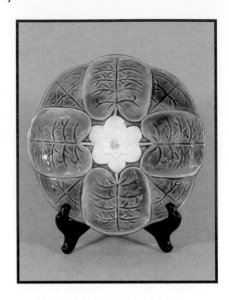

POND LILY PLATE. 9" d.

RUNNING STAG AND DOG PLATE. 8" d. Nicely embossed floral and picket
fence design surrounds this outdoors hunting scene.

SCALLOPED EDGED DOGWOOD PLATE. Approx. 8" d. This beautiful and colorful plate was unmarked but was obviously made by one of the major English potteries. Unfortunately, I sold this piece some time ago and neglected to record the exact measurements, so in these cases I am giving an approximate diameter.

SEAWEED OYSTER PLATE. 10¼" d. Probably American.

SHELL AND CORAL CAKE PLATE. 11" d.

STRAWBERRIES AND LEAVES PLATE. 8¾" d.

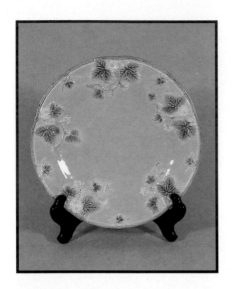

STRAWBERRY BLOSSOMS PLATE. 8"
d. Probably George Jones.

SUNFLOWER OYSTER PLATE. 10" d. Another unusual oyster plate,
this time with sunflowers in the indentations.

TRENTON-TYPE BIRD PLATE. 8¼" d.
Attributed to the Eureka Pottery Co.,
Trenton, NJ.

TWO PARROTS ON A BRANCH
PLATE. 8½" d.

WATER LILY PLATE. 9" d. These pretty plates make a
fabulous table setting if you can put together a set. The
big problem in assembling a large quantity of these is
that the white lily blossom in the center usually has a lot
of wear with the clay showing through the glaze. Our
ancestors used them a lot also!

WEDGWOOD BASKETWEAVE BOR-
DER PLATE. 9" d. Impressed
Wedgwood.

WEDGWOOD BIRD AND FAN PLATE. 9" d. Three wonderfully colorful birds and three stylized fans decorate this beautiful Wedgwood pattern.

WEDGWOOD CHRYSANTHEMUM PLATE. 9" d. Impressed Wedgwood.

WEDGWOOD CRANE PLATE. 9" d. A reticulated edge with simulated basketweave, as well as the long necked crane, distinguishes this plate.

WEDGWOOD DOLPHIN OYSTER PLATE. 9" d. Quite a gaudy and effective departure for Wedgwood. There is a dolphin between each shell. Of course, the swirls represent waves.

WEDGWOOD DOLPHIN OYSTER PLATE. 9¼" d. Impressed Wedgwood with the English Registry mark.

WEDGWOOD FISH PLATE. 9" d.

WEDGWOOD LOBSTER AND VEGETABLES PLATE. 8¾" d. Impressed Wedgwood.

WEDGWOOD OCTAGONAL EDGE PLATE. 9" d.

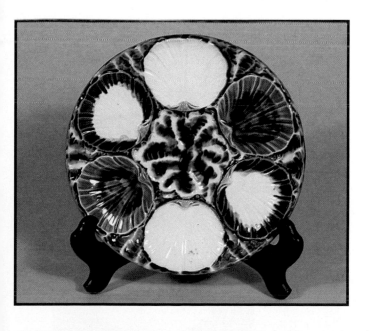

WEDGWOOD MINIATURE OYSTER PLATE. 7" d. This is much smaller than the usual oyster plate; effective coloration with the dark blue of the ocean waves.

WEDGWOOD RE-TICULATED BORDER PLATE. 8¾" d.

WEDGWOOD SCALLOPED EDGE PLATE WITH CLASSICAL SCENE. Approx. 8" d.

WEDGWOOD SHELL PLATE. 8½" d.

WEDGWOOD SHELL PLATE. 9" d. This plate is part of a larger set which included a platter. Coloration will vary.

WILD ROSE PLATE. 8¾" d. Also came in a platter.

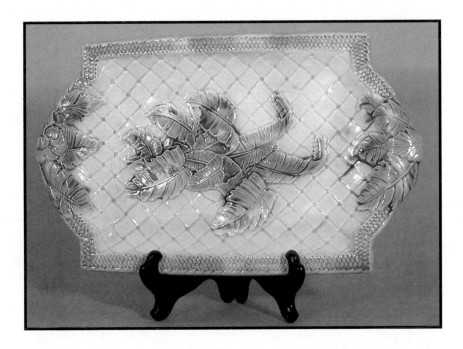

BANANA LEAVES PLATTER. 14" l. Potted in a variety of sizes and colors.

BANANA LEAVES AND BOWS PLATTER. 14½" l.

BAMBOO AND BASKETWEAVE PLATTER. 10½" d. A lush turquoise background with pink bows accenting the handles and an all-over bamboo leaf and blossom design makes this one of the most attractive platters I have had. Majolica at its best!

BAMBOO AND BOW PLATTER. 13" l.

BARREL STAVES AND FLORAL PLATTER. 10" d.

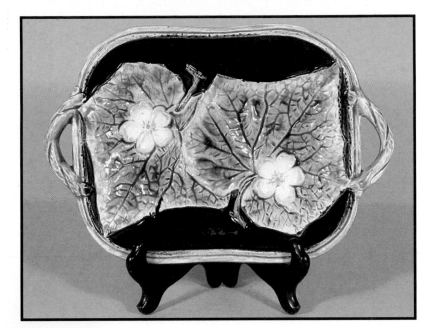

BEGONIA AND FLORAL OPEN HANDLED PLATTER.
11½" l.

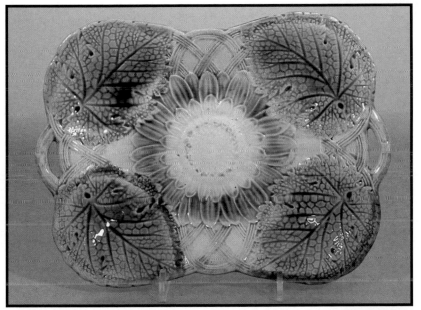

BEGONIA CORNERED PLATTER. Approx. 11" l.

BEGONIA LEAF PLATTER. 13" l.

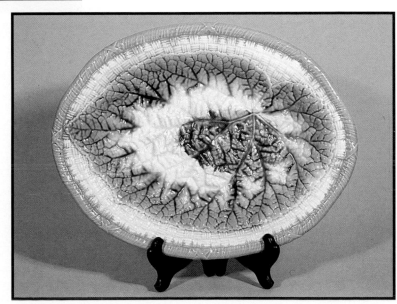

BEGONIA ON BARK PLATTER. 12¼" l. Look for this platter also in a banana leaf pattern.

BIRD AND FAN OVAL PLATTER. 14" l.

BLACKBERRY PLATTER. 14" l.

CIRCULAR BANANA LEAF PLATTER.
12" d.

CLIFTON DECOR BLACKBERRY PLATTER. 13" d. Clifton Decor mark. See mark No. 11.

COBALT CENTERED PICKET FENCE PLATTER. 14" l.

DIAMOND SHAPED FLORAL PLATTER. 12" l.

DRAGONFLY ON LEAF PLATTER. 11" l.

ETRUSCAN SHELL CAKE PLATTER. 13½" l.

FAN AND DRAGONFLY PLATTER. 10½" l.

FERN AND BASKETWEAVE EDGE PLATTER. 11¼" l.

FISH PLATTER. 14" l. An unusual shape and well placed fish distinguish the piece. Definitely English.

FISH AND CORAL WITH WAVES PLATTER. 13" l. The overall shape and the waves on the outer edge are a direct copy of a Wedgwood piece.

FLORAL AND BASKETWEAVE PLATTER. 11" l.

FLYING CRANE AND WATER LILY PLATTER. 10½" d. Produced in a variety of pieces. Includes vases, cups and saucers, luncheon plates, fruit dishes, and a small bowl and milk pitcher.

GEOMETRIC PLATTER WITH STRIPES AND DAISY HANDLES. 13" l.

GRAPE VINE PLATTER. 13" d. The cobalt center really sets off this impressive looking platter with red grapes and green and brown leaves.

HOLDCROFT CATTAIL AND FISH PLATTER. 25" l. I am sure Holdcroft was proud to place his signature on this masterful fish platter. The edges have large figural cattails.

HOLDCROFT RECTANGULAR PLATTER. 13½" l. Impressed J. Holdcroft.

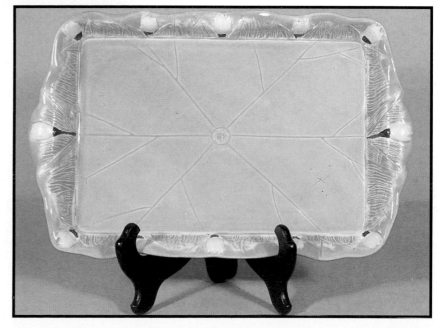

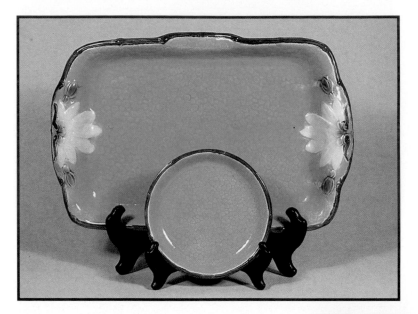

HOLDCROFT WATER LILY PLATTER AND INDIVIDUAL DISHES. 14" platter and 6" dishes. Holdcroft marked this set with his signature. Stylistic water lilies grace the handles and a thin bamboo rim surrounds all the pieces in the set.

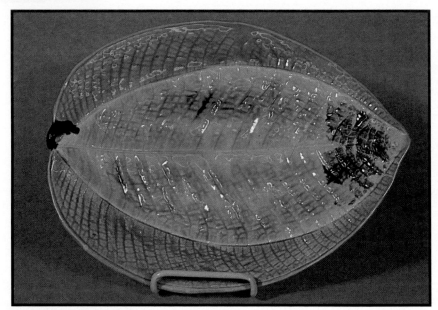

LEAF PLATTER. 13" l.

LEAF AND FLORAL OVAL PLATTER. 15" l.

LEAVES AND FERN PLATTER. 12" l.

MOTTLED CENTER OVAL PLATTER. 14" l.

MOTTLED CENTER RASPBERRY PATTERN PLATTER.
11¾" l.

OVAL FAN AND BUTTERFLY PLATTER. 13¼" l. Impressed shield mark.

OVAL FERN, FLORAL AND BOW PLATTER. 14" l. Attributed to Banks & Thorley, Hanley, England.

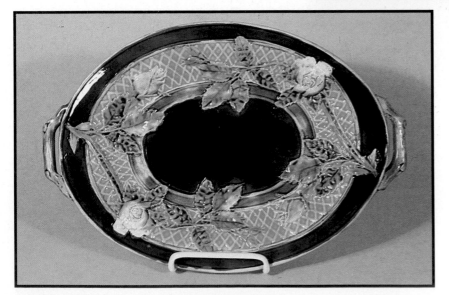

ROSE ON BASKETWEAVE PLATTER. 13" d.

SCALLOPED EDGE DOG AND DOGHOUSE PLATTER. 11" l.

SHELL, SEAWEED AND OCEAN WAVES PLATTER. 13½" l.

STRAWBERRY AND BOW PLATTER. 13½" l. Also plates and teapots.

SUNFLOWER PLATTER. 12½" l. English Registry mark. Attributed to Wardle & Co., Hanley.

SWAN HANDLED PLATTER. 13" l. If you look closely, you can see that the handles are swans with wings outstretched – a very beautiful variation on a bird theme!

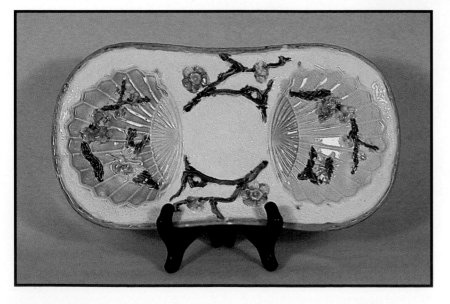

WARDLE BIRD AND FAN TEAPOT PLATTER. 12½" l. English Registry mark. You can collect a large series of the Wardle Bird and Fan pattern. This is one of the more rare pieces. The teapot would sit in the center of the tray.

WATER LILY PLATTER AND DESSERT DISHES.
Platter, 13½" l.; dessert dish, 5¼" x 4¼".

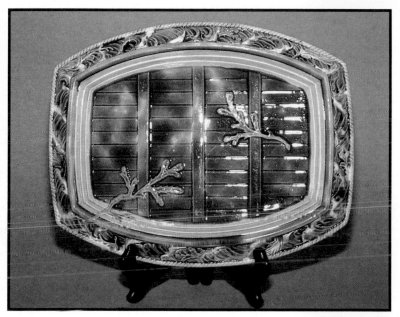

WEDGWOOD BOAT PLATTER. Approx. 14" l. Modeled to
resemble a boat in water with seaweed falling in over the side
as if one were looking down from overhead.

WEDGWOOD FRUIT PLATTER AND 12 PLATES.
Platter, 15½"; plates, 7" d.

WEDGWOOD ORIENTAL PLATTER. Approx. 13" l. This pattern was also done in a plate with a turquoise background.

WEDGWOOD SHELL FISH PLATTER. 23" l. This is one of the most beautiful pieces of Wedgwood I have seen. It can also be found with a white background.

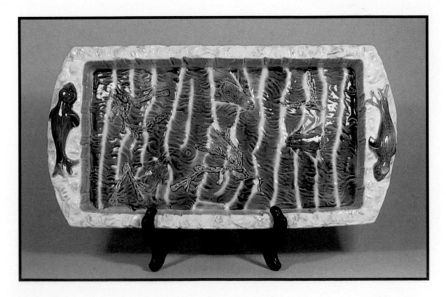

WEDGWOOD SWIMMING SEAL PLATTER. 17" l. A nice addition to Wedgwood's nautical themes is this whimsical platter with seals frolicking amid the ocean waves.

WHITE LILAC OVAL LOBED PLATTER. 13" d.

WILD ROSE PLATTER WITH EYELET HANDLES.

BEGONIA CENTERED "EAT THY BREAD WITH THANKFULNESS" BREAD TRAY. 13" l. The motto is in raised letters around the border. These "motto bread trays" form a distinct collecting category.

CORN BREAD TRAY. 12" l.

"EAT THY BREAD WITH THANKFULNESS" WHEAT PATTERN BREAD TRAY. 13" l.

ETRUSCAN BEGONIA LEAF TRAY. 9" l. Also produced in an 8" version. Coloration varies. These were originally intended as pickle dishes.

ETRUSCAN OAK FRUIT TRAY. 12" l. This monumental bowl was produced by Griffin, Smith and Hill, Phoenixville, Pennsylvania and bears the circular Etruscan Majolica mark. Also with a white background.

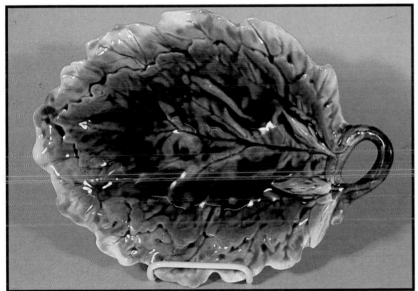

ETRUSCAN OAK LEAF BREAD TRAY. 13" d. The large oak leaf bread tray used to be fairly common to find but now I hardly ever see one. Look for nice bright pink edge coloration and good condition. They are especially hard to find in good shape. Check the handle for repair. I have even seen them for sale with the handle completely broken off.

FIELDING FAN ICE CREAM TRAY. 14½" l. Impressed English Registry mark and FIELDING.

GEORGE JONES PALM AND GRAPE LEAF TRAY. 8" d. The colors on this are spectacular – a lovely small tray by George Jones.

GRAPE LEAF RELISH TRAY. 8" l.

OVAL GERANIUM RELISH TRAY. 8" l. The colors here are so similar to Wedgwood. However, I believe it may be American, probably Clifton by Chesapeake Pottery Co.

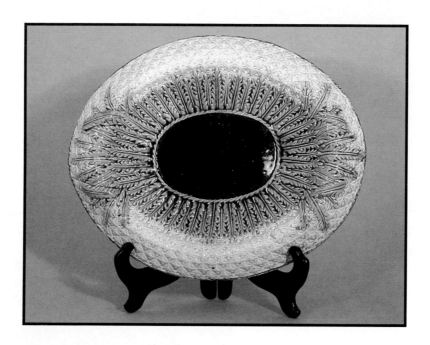

PINEAPPLE BREAD TRAY. 13" l. Probably Wardle & Co., Hanley, England.

POND LILY BREAD TRAY. 13" l.

SQUARE FLORAL PIN TRAY. 5¼" d.

TWIN SHELL ON WAVES BREAD TRAY. 14" l.

WARDLE'S BAMBOO AND FERN BREAD TRAY. 13" l.

"WASTE NOT—WANT NOT" BUTTERFLY BREAD TRAY. 13½" l.

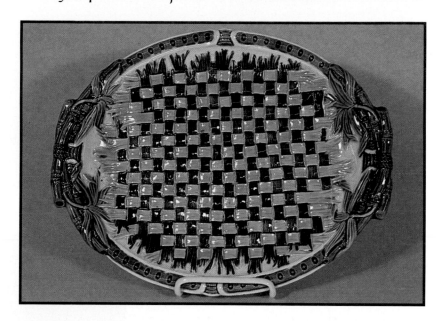

WEDGWOOD BASKETWEAVE CLOTH ON BREAD TRAY. 12" d. A realistic rendition of a breadcloth lays across this pretty tray.

WEDGWOOD ONION & PICKLE RELISH TRAY. 8" l.

WEDGWOOD ONION AND PICKLE RELISH TRAY. 8" l.

L. to R. All approx. 3" d. BEGONIA LEAF ON BASKETWEAVE BUTTER PAT. POINTED LEAF SHAPED BUTTER PAT. MORNING GLORY ON NAPKIN BUTTER PAT.

L. to R. ETRUSCAN BEGONIA LEAF BUTTER PAT. 3¾" l.; ETRUSCAN SUNFLOWER UNDERPLATE. 5" d.; ETRUSCAN WICKER AND BEGONIA BUTTER PAT. 3" d.

L. to R. All approx. 3" d. ETRUSCAN "LATER-STYLE" GERANIUM BUTTER PAT. FIELDING BUTTERFLY BUTTER PAT. Impressed Fielding mark. ETRUSCAN GERANIUM LEAF "OLD STYLE" BUTTER PAT. This older version of the Etruscan geranium leaf is much thicker and has a distinct "ruffled" effect which the later version lacks.

L. to R. All approx. 3" d. ETRUSCAN SMILAX BUTTER PAT. The smilax pattern is rare. ETRUSCAN PANSY BUTTER PAT. ETRUSCAN POND LILY BUTTER PAT.

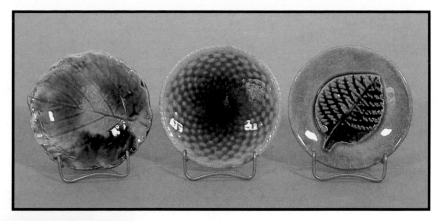

L. to R. All approx. 3" d. LEAF SHAPED BUTTER PAT. ETRUSCAN WICKER BUTTER PAT. TWO-TONED LEAF BUTTER PAT.

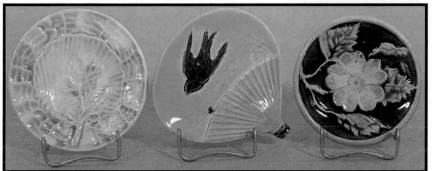

L. to R. All approx. 3" d. SHELL AND SEAWEED BUTTER PAT. This is a copy of the Wedgwood version. FAN AND SWALLOW BUTTER PAT. CO-BALT FLORAL BUTTER PAT.

L. to R. All approx. 3" d. THREE GREEN LEAF BUT-TER PAT. WEDGWOOD SHELL AND SEAWEED BUTTER PAT. FLORAL BUTTER PAT.

L. to R. All approx. 3" d. WEDGWOOD HORSESHOE BUTTER PAT. Impressed Wedgwood. WEDGWOOOD GREEN LEAF BUTTER PAT. Impressed Wedgwood. GREEN LEAF BUTTER PAT.

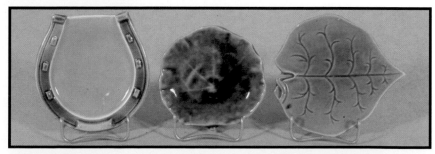

L. to R. All 3" d. WEDGWOOD SHELL AND SEAWEED BUTTER PAT. WEDGWOOD ASTOR BUTTER PAT. ETRUSCAN LEAF ON PLATE BUTTER PAT.

BAMBOO AND BASKETWEAVE CUP AND SAUCER. Saucer 6" d. Colorful red prunus blossoms lay over a basketweave background with green bamboo leaf accents.

BAMBOO AND BASKETWEAVE CUP AND SAUCER. Saucer 6" d. Part of a large series in this pattern, I think I even remember once owning the cup with a figural butterfly handle. Probably very difficult to produce and often broken.

BAMBOO AND FLORAL CUP AND SAUCER. Saucer approx. 6" d.

BASKETWEAVE AND FLORAL CUP AND SAUCER. Saucer approx. 6" d. Basketweave background with a white blossom and green leaves.

BASKETWEAVE AND FLORAL TEAPOT AND SUGAR BOWL. L. to R., approx. 6" h. and 4" h.

BIRD SUGAR AND CREAM PITCHER. L. to R., 3½" h. and 2¼" h.

BIRD AND FAN COBALT SUGAR BOWL. 4½" h. Produced in a tea set, also with a yellow background.

BLUE FLORAL SUGAR AND CREAM PITCHER. L. to R., 4" h. and 3" h.

BOW AND LEAF CREAM PITCHER. 3¼" h. English Registry mark.

CHICK ON NEST TEAPOT. Approx. 6" h. The little chick forms the finial while the teapot is a twig and leaf entwined nest.

CLIFTON DECOR BLACKBERRY TEAPOT. Approx. 6" h. Made by David Francis Haynes who purchased the Chesapeake Pottery Co. in Baltimore, Maryland in 1880. Marked "Clifton Decor." This was the first pattern produced by David Haynes. For a copious sampling of pieces produced in this pattern see page 57 of Charles Rebert's book, *American Majolica*.

COBALT BIRD TEAPOT. 6¾" h. This unusual teapot has a long necked bird on each side. On the spout, one side has a bird and the other a butterfly. Similar in design to the Etruscan bird teapot, this example shows a design refinement – when tea is served from the Etruscan teapot it spills out between the body and the lid. The lid on this teapot is only a small rectangular section under the handle – the tea stays in!

CORN TEAPOT AND SUGAR BOWL. L. to R., 6" h. and 6½" h. Most beautiful and rare!

DRUM SHAPED TEAPOT. 9" h.

DRUM SHAPED TWIG FOOTED TEA SET. L. to R., 6" h., 6½" h., 3¾" h.

ETRUSCAN ALBINO TEAPOT AND SUGAR BOWL. L. to R. 5½" h. and 5" h. Only the sugar bowl bears the circular Etruscan Majolica mark.

ETRUSCAN ALBINO SHELL AND SEAWEED SPOONER AND CREAM PITCHER. L. to R. 3¼" h., and 3½" h. Unmarked. Only about one in ten albino pieces bears the Etruscan Majolica mark.

ETRUSCAN BAMBOO TEA SET AND PLATE. Plate, 8" d. L. to R. Sugar bowl, 6" h., teapot, 6¾" h., cream pitcher, 4½" h., spooner (rare), 4¼" h. One of the "Big Three" patterns produced by Griffin, Smith and Hill (others are Shell and Seaweed and Cauliflower), this was made in a full tea set including waste bowl and covered butter dish. Only one size plate was produced.

ETRUSCAN BAMBOO CUP AND SAUCER. Saucer, 6" d. You can collect the whole tea set including small tea plates in this pattern. In addition to the usual three-piece tea set there is a spoon holder and covered butter dish if you can find them. I have had them all at one time but to my regret I sold them.

ETRUSCAN BIRD AND IRIS THREE PIECE TEA SET. L. to R. 5" h., 6 " h., and 3¾" h. The lid to the teapot here is not the correct color. Scarce. Also with a blue background.

ETRUSCAN CAULIFLOWER CUP AND SAUCER. 7" d. This cup and saucer is part of the Etruscan cauliflower series which also includes a tea set and two sizes of plates. The set pictured is very rare. They will likely be the last pieces of the set to be found.

ETRUSCAN CAULIFLOWER TEAPOT AND SUGAR BOWL. Teapot 4¼" to top of spout. A classic Griffin, Smith, and Hill pattern, this was adopted from a Wedgwood design.

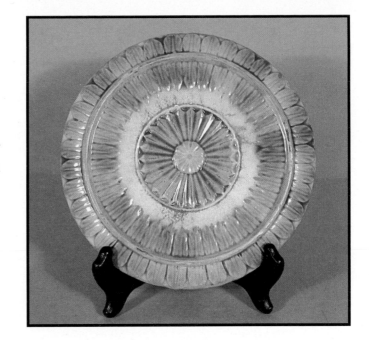

ETRUSCAN CONVENTIONAL TEAPOT STAND. 7" d. Small protrusions on the back hold this up off the table. Very rare.

ETRUSCAN SHELL AND SEAWEED CREAM PITCHER AND SUGAR BOWL. L. to R. 5" h. and 3½" h. This is the cream pitcher to the coffee set. There is one size smaller which goes with the tea set. The double handled covered sugar bowl is rare.

ETRUSCAN SHELL AND SEAWEED CUP AND SAUCER, COFFEE POT, TEAPOT AND PLATES. L. to R. Plate, 8" d. Teapot, 6" h. Plate, 9" d. (rare). Coffee pot, 6¼" h. Teacup and saucer, saucer is 6" d. There is also a coffee sized cup and saucer with a 7" d. saucer which is more scarce than the teacup size. Beware of coffee cups with teacup (6" d.) saucers!

ETRUSCAN SHELL AND SEAWEED MUSTACHE CUP. 8" d. A rare find! Be careful that you also get the large 8" saucer which is the correct size. Of course, even without the saucer, it is not an item to be passed up.

ETRUSCAN WASTE BOWL WITH TEAPOT. 5" d. waste bowl. This is the only one I have ever had or seen. Another Cauliflower teapot can be seen on page 148 so that you can see the difference in glaze color. This one has one side of the leaf in pink and the other in gray. It is a challenge to collect your complete tea set with all the coloring the same. Note the waste bowl has pink edging on both sides. The teapot of page 148 shows the leaf done only in green. Were there any other color combinations in this pattern?

ETRUSCAN WILD ROSE COVERED SUGAR BOWL. 3¾"
d. Marked "MI3" underneath. Made by Griffin, Smith and
Hill.

FIELDING FAN CUP AND SAUCER. 7"
d. saucer. The cup has the English
Registry mark and the saucer is impressed FIELDING. Also in a smaller
version.

FIELDING HUMMINGBIRD COFFEE
POT. 9" h. English Registry mark. Also
in a pitcher.

FIELDING SHELL CREAM PITCHER AND SUGAR
BOWL. L. to R. Approx. 4" h. and approx. 5" h. English
Registry mark. Impressed FIELDING.

FLORAL CUP AND SAUCER. 5¼" d. saucer.

FLORAL SUGAR AND CREAM PITCHER. L. to R. 3½" h. and 3" h.

FLORAL SUGAR AND CREAM PITCHER.

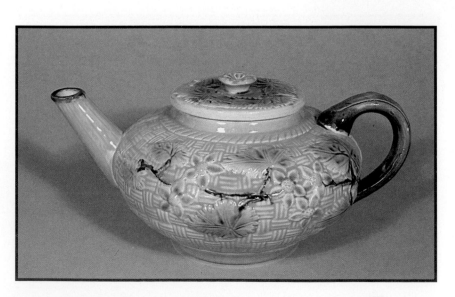

FLORAL AND BASKETWEAVE TEAPOT. 5" h.

FLORAL AND BASKETWEAVE TEAPOT. 4½" h. The metal lid adds to the value of this teapot.

FLYING CRANE TEAPOT. 6¾" h.

HOLDCROFT CHINAMAN ON A COCONUT TEAPOT. 7" h. This could either be a melon or coconut. The chinaman's head comes off to reveal the opening for the water. Any of these figural teapots are rare and valuable.

HOLDCROFT MELON SUGAR BOWL AND CREAM PITCHER. 4" h. and 2"h. These match the pattern on the teapot on page 155. The background color on the teapot is brown and these can probably be found also in that color.

HOLLY AND BERRIES TEAPOT. 6" h. This design includes a bark spout and handle.

ISLE OF MAN THREE-LEGGED FIGURAL TEAPOT. 8" h. This very unusual piece is in the shape of a three-legged man. The head lifts off to pour in the water and the tea pours through the leg at the back. It is marked "W. BROUGHTON, SO. DUKE ST. DOUGLAS." It seems to have been an advertising piece. "Douglas" is the capital of the ISLE OF MAN, which is located off Great Britain in the Irish Sea. This piece has value from an historical perspective, and as a desirable lidded figural piece.

IVY COVERED COTTAGE SUGAR BOWL AND
CREAM PITCHER. 3" h. and 4" h. This unusual figural
design also comes in a teapot. The pitcher comes in
more than one size.

LEAF AND BOW SUGAR BOWL. 4" h. See the
companion cream pitcher on page 144.

MELON WITH BUMPS TEAPOT. 6½" h. Also in a
cream colored background.

MINTON'S CHINAMAN TEAPOT. 6" h. Another lovely example of Minton's way with figurals. Again, here the head lifts off.

MINTON MONKEY FIGURAL TEAPOT. 7" h. A desirable Minton figural piece.

PARROT ON A BRANCH SUGAR BOWL. 5½" h.

PEWTER TOPPED TEAPOT. 6" h. The pewter top adds value.

PINEAPPLE CUP AND SAUCER AND SUGAR BOWL. L. to R. 4¾" d. and 5½" d.

PINEAPPLE CUP AND SAUCER. 7" d. Look for other pieces in the pineapple series, such as the tea set and various size plates.

POND LILY MUSTACHE CUP. 3¾" d. across top of cup. Extremely rare. Just try putting together a large collection of Majolica mustache cups! This lily pattern was very popular.

PYRAMID TEA SET. Teapot approx. 6½" h. Creamer approx. 3½" h. Sugar is missing lid here. These timely pieces were made to commemorate the obelisk in Central Park in New York City.

ROBIN RED BREAST CHILD'S MINIATURE THREE-PIECE TEA SET. Teapot 3½" h. Very rare to find this child's tea set intact with all three pieces including the covers for the sugar and teapot. I wonder if there were tiny cups and saucers to match? Let me know!

ROSE AND ROPE THREE-PIECE TEA SET AND PLATTER. Platter 15½" l. Tea set, L. to R.: 4½" h., 6½" h., and 3½" h. This pattern was also done in plates and compotes.

ROSE AND ROPE CUP AND SAUCER. Saucer 5½" d. Beautiful shade of lavender lining. If you become a real connoisseur, you will come to prefer a certain shade of lavender interior. This one produced by Griffin, Smith, and Hill is my favorite.

ROSE AND ROPE SUGAR BOWL. 4" h. Here is the sugar bowl, this time in a brown background.

SAMUEL LEAR SUNFLOWER AND CLASSICAL URN MUSTACHE CUP AND SAUCER. Saucer 6½" d. Samuel Lear of Hanley, England registered this design on August 27, 1881, patent #369202. Also in plates, platters and cakestands.

SAMUEL LEAR SUNFLOWER AND CLASSICAL URN TEAPOT. 6" h. This teapot joins a large family of pieces in the urn and sunflower pattern.

SEASHELL AND OCEAN WAVES CREAM PITCHER. 4" h. Belongs to a large family of shell and wave pieces.

SHELL CUP AND SAUCER. Demitasse size. This irresistible shell pattern cup and saucer is new to me. I have never seen any other pieces in this pattern. All Majolica cup and saucer sets are rare and they make a particularly nice collecting specialty.

SHELL AND SEAWEED SUGAR BOWL WITH FISH FINIAL AND HANDLES. Approx. 5" h. High level of craftsmanship and design.

STRAWBERRY AND BOW TEAPOT. 6" h. A strawberry on the finial and on the handle, this pattern was also done in a platter and dessert plates.

TREE BARK AND FOOTED THREE-PIECE TEA SET. L. to R. 4½" h., 6½" h., and 3" h. Also look for a pitcher in this pattern. Nicely detailed spout in the form of a tree branch. Intricately shaped finial.

TURQUOISE BASKETWEAVE AND FLORAL THREE PIECE TEA SET. L. to R. 4½" h., 6" h., and 3½" h.

WARDLE BAMBOO AND FERN MUS-TACHE CUP AND SAUCER. 7" d. This is a beautiful example of a rare mustache cup. The lavender lining is particularly nice.

WARDLE'S FERN AND BAMBOO CUP AND SAUCER AND SUGAR BOWL. Produced by Wardle & Co. of Hanley, these bear the English Registry mark and are part of a large series of pieces.

WATER LILY TEAPOT. Approx. 4" h. Part of a large family of the water lily pattern.

WATER LILY COFFEE CUP AND SAUCER. Saucer 6½" d.

WEDGWOOD SHELL AND SEAWEED TEA-POT. 7" h.

WILD ROSE AND TRELLIS TEACUP. 2½" h. We are missing the saucer here as so often happens. Don't hesitate to pick up these incomplete teacups. The next piece you find just may be the saucer.

BIRD IN FLIGHT AND POND LILY VASE.
Approx. 10" h. Also comes in a cobalt
background.

BIRD ON TREE BRANCH. 7" h.

CLASSICAL HARP VASE. 6" h. A very graceful harp with classical woman forms a small bud vase.

ETRUSCAN CELERY VASE. 8¾" h. One of the most lovely of the Griffin, Smith, and Hill pieces and very, very rare.

FOOTED BIRD VASE. 7" h. Magnificent workmanship detail and coloring. Probably produced by one of the major English potters – possibly Copeland or Minton.

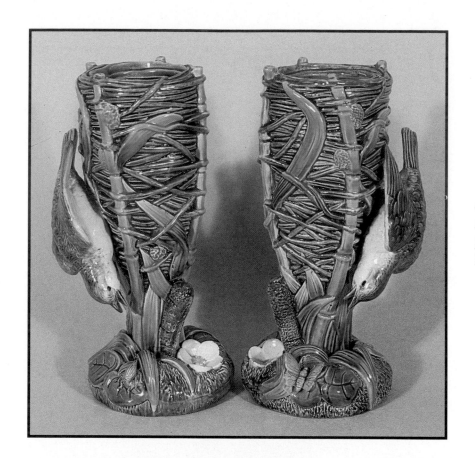

GEORGE JONES BIRD'S NEST AND BIRD VASES. 8" h. These are truly the most outstanding pair of Jones vases! The detail in the bird's nests is unbelievable.

GEORGE JONES CLASSICAL PUTTI VASES. 8" h. Lilac drapery enhances this classical pair balancing bud vases on their heads.

GEORGE JONES CLASSICAL PUTTI WITH NAUTILUS SHELLS AND VASES. 6" h. Here is another pair of George Jones' putti, this time in a nautical setting!

LILAC THROATED SONG BIRD VASES. 6" h. What could be prettier than these two little birds and their trumpet-shaped flowers forming a bud vase!

LION FOOTED COBALT VASE. 9" h.

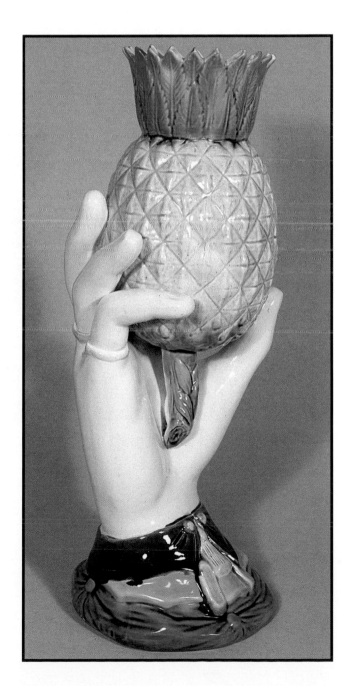

PINEAPPLE HAND VASE. 13" h. If you compare this to the vase on the next page, you will notice that this has much more detail. The size also is just stupendous – this has to be seen to be believed. Notice the tassel at the wrist and the ring on the fingers. English Registry mark.

PINEAPPLE HAND VASE. 7¼" h. Very rare Victorian oddity. The hand even sports a cuff with tassel.

RARE AND UNUSUAL CRANE AND PRUNUS VASE. 6" h. There is always an exception to every rule! The photo below shows the back with its applied flowers. We like to say that true Victorian Majolica does not *usually* have applied decoration such as flowers. Quite rare.

TRIPLET HANDLED URN GROUP. 5" to 7" h. Each in this lovely trio has an intense turquoise lining. They are unsigned, but the coloring is so reminiscent of Brownfield.

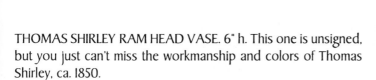

SONGBIRD WITH TRIPLE THROATED VASE. 8" h.

THOMAS SHIRLEY RAM HEAD VASE. 6" h. This one is unsigned, but you just can't miss the workmanship and colors of Thomas Shirley, ca. 1850.

BOY AND GIRL CANDLESTICKS. 7" h. Probably French.

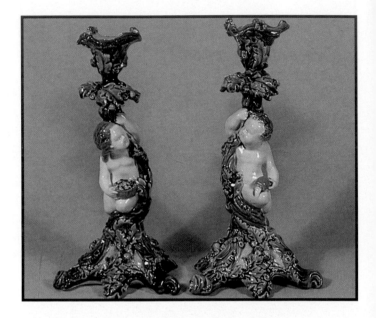

WEDGWOOD FIGURAL CANDLESTICKS. II" h. These are very rare and very beautiful; the value is enhanced because they are a pair.

WORCESTER DOLPHIN CANDLESTICK. 4" h. Notice the similarity to the Worcester piece on page 34. Worcester Majolica is very hard to find. The coloration and the intensity of the glaze is a little different from most Victorian Majolica.

BOY RIDING A DOLPHIN POND LILY CENTERPIECE. 12" h. White central lily flower surrounded by large green lily pad. Beautiful from any angle.

DEER HEAD CIGARETTE HOLDER. 5" h.

ETRUSCAN SHELL AND SEAWEED CUSPIDOR. 7" h. Another one of the rare Etruscan cuspidors; this one will be needed for cuspidor collections in general and to complete Shell and Seaweed collections as well.

ETRUSCAN SUNFLOWER CUSPIDOR. 7" h. This is a very rare Etruscan piece. The Sunflower cuspidor was also produced with a blue background.

ETRUSCAN SUNFLOWER CUSPIDOR. 6" h. Very rare.

FAN CUSPIDOR. 6½" h.

FLORAL CUSPIDOR. 5½" h.

FLORAL CUSPIDOR. 7" h.

FLORAL AND BASKETWEAVE CUSPIDOR. 7" h.

SHELL AND SEAWEED CUSPIDOR. 6" h.

TENUOUS MAJOLICA SHELL CUSPIDOR. 5" h. Although it is not as gaily colored as most Victorian Majolica, this cuspidor is among the rarest of American Majolica. I never thought I would see a piece with the elusive "TENUOUS MAJOLICA " mark, but here it is. See photo of the mark in the Marks section.

MORNING GLORY EGG BASKET WITH EGG CUPS. 6" h. Egg baskets are hard to find, particularly with all the egg cups intact.

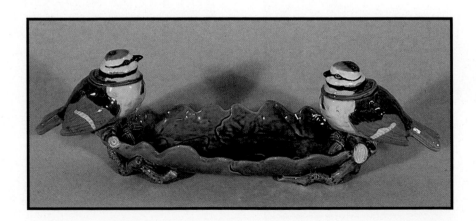

MINTON TWIN BIRD INKWELL. 9" l. Surely this is a lovely and valuable piece by Minton. Each little bird's head lifts to reveal the inkwells.

POND LILY JARDINIERE. 8" h.

WEDGWOOD BLACKBERRY JARDINIERE. 10" h. Wedgwood called this the "Bramble" garden pot. It was modeled by Birks and registered in 1868.

WARDLE BIRD AND FAN COVERED MATCHBOX. 4" l. I overpaid dearly once for a collection of over 100 pieces (many severely repaired) purchased sight unseen by mail, and was rewarded by receiving this lovely and rare little matchbox. The bottom is ridged to strike the match. That is how you can tell these little covered boxes are matchboxes, and not hairpin holders. You can also see this rare matchbox, attributed to Eureka Pottery, pictured on page 63 of Rebert's *American Majolica*. This may be true of some of the pieces pictured, but the photograph includes numerous patterns of the "Bird and Fan" genre and this particular pattern has been attributed to Wardle through the English Registry mark on the bottom of the pitcher of the same pattern. The matchbox is unmarked. I have never sold this or seen one for sale so the value would be whatever one is willing to pay.

ELEPHANT MATCH HOLDER. 8" h. Probably English.

HOLDCROFT DRUMMER BOY MATCH HOLDER. 3" h. A uniquely designed piece by Holdcroft; the bottom of one upturned foot is ridged for a match striker.

STANDING MONKEY WEARING LOINCLOTH MATCH HOLDER. 7¾" h.

FLORAL AND FERN PLANTER WITH GROTESQUE HEADS. 7" h. Unsigned and unusual.

GEORGE JONES DAISY AND BANANA LEAF PLANTER. 10" h. This has a lovely lavender lining. Also look for a cheese keeper and umbrella stand in this pattern.

GEORGE JONES EGYPTIAN STYLE PLANTER. 7" h. The cobalt blue coloring and the stately geometric Egyptian motif sets this apart from most Jones pieces.

MINTON CATTAIL PLANTER WITH UNDER DISH. 6" h. A beautifully simple piece with lavish coloring.

PICKET FENCE AND RASPBERRY PATTERN PLANTER. 8" h. Lavender lining.

ETRUSCAN SALT AND PEPPER SHAKERS. 4" h. This pair is in the coral pattern. Impressed "LI5."

WEDGWOOD SALT DIP. 5" h. A small child holds a wicker basket.

ASPARAGUS SERVER ON OCEAN WAVES. 11" l.

FIGURAL DEER'S HEAD SWEETMEAT SERVER. 4½" h. Most beautiful with very excellent workmanship. Possibly Copeland.

GEORGE JONES STRAWBERRY SERVER WITH SPOON. 13" l. This has two separate inserts, one for cream and one for sugar. The serving spoon is very rare.

GEORGE JONES STRAWBERRY SERVER. 10" d. This is a graceful treatment of the classic theme. It is unusual for the single cup to be attached to the center of the bowl.

MINTON ASPARAGUS SERVER. 10¼" l., 8¾" w. Impressed MINTON.

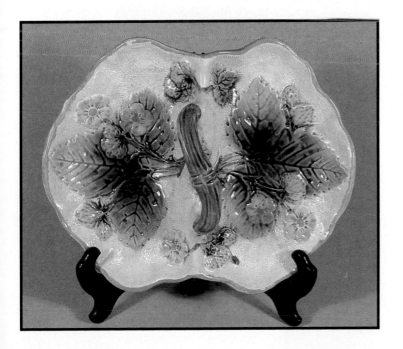

RUSTIC HANDLED SERVER. 10½" l. Decorated with strawberries, leaves and blossoms. A perfect example of the motif suggesting the intended use.

STRAWBERRY SERVER WITH INDI-VIDUAL SUGAR BOWL AND CREAM PITCHER. 10¼" l., 8" w. These are rare and desirable pieces particularly with the separate sugar bowl and cream pitcher intact. They fit into the circular wells in the server. Almost exactly like the Etruscan strawberry server, although this example is unmarked.

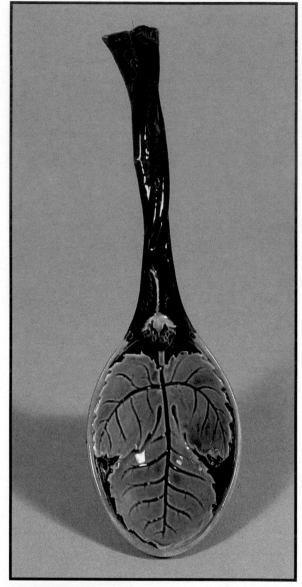

HOLDCROFT STRAWBERRY SERVING SPOON. 5" l. These spoons originally went with the strawberry servers – very hard to find.

UNUSUAL FLORAL SOAP DISH. 4" d. This is molded in one piece and there is a small hole for the water to drain out.

COLLECTION OF SPOON HOLDERS. L. to R. 5", 4½", 7½", 5¼", 4". You will recognize some of your favorite patterns here such as the water lily (third and fourth from left) and Wardle's Bird and Fan (second from left). Spoon holders are rare. I would guess that a great number of you have a complete tea set in a certain pattern, but did not know the spoon holder existed. Prices here are variable, depending upon the pattern, and how badly you want it.

FAN SPOON HOLDER. 5" h.

CHICK TOOTHPICK. 4" h.

GEORGE JONES TRIVET. 7" d. This is an attractive trivet in Jones' colors.

ETRUSCAN TUMBLER. 4" h. This rare Etruscan piece has a pattern very similar to the one on the Baseball Players pitcher, minus the players. Look for a large pitcher in this pattern as well.

HOLDCROFT ARTIST-SIGNED MONUMENTAL BIRD UMBRELLA STAND. Approx. three feet tall. This extraordinary piece is unbelievable. This bird is just huge and the detailing extremely fine. It is signed by the artist near the base, "T. Fay, Sculptor."

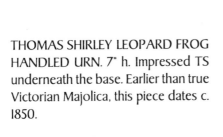

THOMAS SHIRLEY LEOPARD FROG HANDLED URN. 7" h. Impressed TS underneath the base. Earlier than true Victorian Majolica, this piece dates c. 1850.

GEORGE JONES WINE CADDY. 13" l. This is certainly one of the most elaborate and intricate Jones pieces. The wheels are attached to a spoke, and actually turn! The sides of the wine holders are reticulated with realistic grape leaves and the little putto in the center is eating a bunch of grapes.

WEDGWOOD WINE COOLER. 10" h. This can be quite a useful and decorative table accent.

BOY RIDING A GOAT. 9" h. The sculptural quality and flowing lines of this figure are just beautiful. Unsigned, but it is certainly by one of the major English potters.

CONCH SHELL ON FIGURAL CORAL.. 4" h.

GEORGE JONES ANGELS ON DOLPHINS. 7" h. Each holds a swirl patterned shell.

MINTON BOY AND GIRL WITH SHELLS. 8" h.

MINTON PUTTI CARRYING SHELL. 8" h. Fine detail and graceful forms distinguish this lovely Minton sculpture.

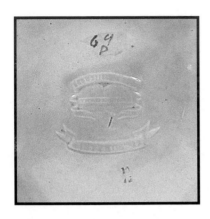

BROWNFIELD & SON "DOUBLE-GLOBE" MARK. Used from 1871 to 1891.

EDWIN BENNETT POTTERY CO. Baltimore, MD. c. 1873.

CHESAPEAKE POTTERY. Baltimore, MD. c. 1880.

W.T. COPELAND (& SONS LTD.) Stoke, England. c. 1847. Impressed "COPELAND" along with the English Registry mark and the name "GILL" which may have been the importer on this particular piece.

ENGLISH REGISTRY MARK AND IMPRESSION "MADE IN ENGLAND," indicating a twentieth century origin.

ETRUSCAN MARK. This is a variation of the Etruscan mark which appears on the bottom of the rare Etruscan sardine box.

S. FIELDING & CO. (LTD.) Stoke, England. c. 1879. The name "FIELD-ING" was impressed in a straight line either with or without the diamond shaped English Registry mark shown here.

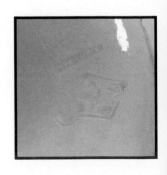

GRIFFIN, SMITH AND HILL. The GSH monogram without the encircling phrase "Etruscan Majolica" as shown next, is considered to be the earlier mark. This mark is always used inside the pedestal on footed pieces, on butter pats, as well as many other pieces.

GRIFFIN, SMITH AND HILL. Phoenixville, PA. 1879–1889.

JOSEPH HOLDCROFT. Longton, England. c. 1865–1906.

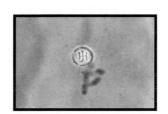

JOSEPH HOLDCROFT. Impressed monogram.

GEORGE JONES. This mark is probably earlier than either of the others. The diamond shaped figure is the English Registry mark.

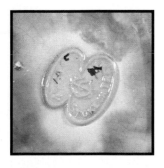

GEORGE JONES. This mark is on an applied pad.

GEORGE JONES & SONS. Stoke, England. c. 1864–1907. The "& Sons" was added to the GJ monogram in 1873.

TENUOUS MAJOLICA. This is the mark on the bottom of the very rare Tenuous Majolica shell cuspidor. It is believed that the mark is American.

WELLSVILLE CHINA CO. Wellsville, OH. c. 1879.

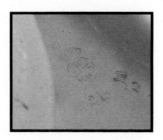

WORCESTER ROYAL PORCELAIN COMPANY LTD. Worcester, England. c. 1862. Impressed crown over circle.

Wedgwood Green Leaf Butter Pat 95.00–110.00
Green Leaf Butter Pat................ 40.00–60.00
Wedgwood Shell/Seaweed Butter Pat .. 225.00–250.00
Wedgwood Astor Butter Pat 125.00–150.00
Etruscan Leaf on Plate Butter Pat....... 125.00–150.00
Page 142
Bamboo/Basketweave Cup/Saucer.... 275.00–300.00
Bamboo/Basketweave Cup/Saucer.... 275.00–300.00
Page 143
Bamboo and Floral Cup and Saucer... 275.00–300.00
Basketweave and Floral Cup/Saucer... 275.00–300.00
Basketweave and Floral Teapot 225.00–275.00
    Sugar Bowl 175.00–200.00
Bird Sugar and Cream Pitcher 300.00–325.00
Page 144
Bird and Fan Cobalt Sugar Bowl 200.00–225.00
Blue Floral Sugar and Cream Pitcher .. 200.00–225.00
Bow and Leaf Cream Pitcher 150.00–165.00
Chick on Nest Teapot 300.00–350.00
Page 145
Clifton Decor Blackberry Teapot 225.00–275.00
Cobalt Bird Teapot 275.00–325.00
Page 146
Corn Teapot 250.00–300.00
    Sugar Bowl 175.00–200.00
Drum Shaped Teapot 375.00–475.00
Drum Shaped Twig Footed Tea Set.... 675.00–775.00
Albino Teapot..................... 250.00–300.00
    Sugar Bowl 175.00–225.00
Page 147
Albino Shell and Seaweed Spooner... 200.00–250.00
Cream Pitcher 200.00–275.00
Etruscan Bamboo Tea Set, Plate 175.00–200.00
    Sugar Bowl, 225.00–250.00; Teapot, 275.00–300.00
    Cr. Pitcher, 200.00–225.00; Spooner, 225.00–275.00
Etruscan Bamboo Cup and Saucer .,,, 225.00–275.00
Page 148
Bird and Iris Three Piece Tea Set..... 700.00–900.00
Cauliflower Cup and Saucer 325.00–375.00
Cauliflower Teapot................. 600.00–700.00
    Sugar Bowl................... 450.00–500.00
Page 149
Eruscan Conventional Teapot Stand ... 325.00–375.00
Shell and Seaweed Cream Pitcher 225.00–275.00
    Sugar Bowl 325.00–375.00
Shell and Seaweed Cup/Saucer....... 325.00–375.00
Coffee Pot, 900.00–1,000.00; Teapot, 900.00–1,000.00;
    Plates, 375.00–425.00, 200.00–250.00
Page 150
Shell and Seaweed Mustache Cup..... 375.00–475.00
Etruscan Waste Bowl 550.00–650.00
Teapot.......................... 700.00–800.00
Page 151
Etruscan Wild Rose Covered Sugar.... 175.00–200.00
Fielding Fan Cup and Saucer......... 250.00–300.00
Fielding Hummingbird Coffee Pot 500.00–600.00
Fielding Shell Cream Pitcher.......... 225.00–275.00
    Sugar Bowl....................... 250.00–300.00
Page 152
Floral Cup and Saucer............... 225.00–275.00
Floral Sugar and Cream Pitcher 225.00–275.00
Floral Sugar and Cream Pitcher 175.00–200.00
Floral and Basketweave Teapot 250.00–300.00
Page 153
Floral and Basketweave Teapot 275.00–325.00
Flying Crane Teapot 250.00–300.00
Chinaman on a Coconut Teapot ... 1,200.00–1,300.00
Page 154
Melon Sugar Bowl/Cream Pitcher, ea... 150.00–225.00

Holly and Berries Teapot............ 225.00–275.00
Isle of Man Figural Teapot........ 1,600.00–2,100.00
Page 155
Ivy Covered Cottage Sugar Bowl....... 175.00–225.00
    Cream Pitcher 175.00–225.00
Leaf and Bow Sugar Bowl............ 150.00–175.00
Melon With Bumps Teapot 350.00–400.00
Page 156
Minton's Chinaman Teapot........ 1,600.00–1,700.00
Minton Monkey Teapot 2,100.00–2,600.00
Parrot on a Branch Sugar Bowl 175.00–200.00
Pewter Topped Teapot.............. 225.00–250.00
Page 157
Pineapple Cup and Saucer 175.00–200.00
    Sugar Bowl 175.00–200.00
Pineapple Cup and Saucer 225.00–250.00
Pond Lily Mustache Cup 350.00–400.00
Page 158
Pyramid Tea Set................... 225.00–250.00
Robin Red Breast Child's Tea Set..... 350.00–450.00
Page 159
Rose and Rope Three-Piece Tea Set .. 375.00–475.00
    Platter....................... 325.00–400.00
Rose and Rope Cup and Saucer 250.00–275.00
Rose and Rope Sugar Bowl.......... 150.00–175.00
Page 160
Samuel Lear Mustache Cup/Saucer ... 425.00–475.00
Samuel Lear Teapot................ 325.00–375.00
Seashell/Ocean Waves Cream Pitcher.. 125.00–150.00
Shell Cup and Saucer 275.00–300.00
Page 161
Shell and Seaweed Sugar Bowl 275.00–325.00
Strawberry and Bow Teapot 500.00–600.00
Tree Bark and Footed Tea Set....... 600.00–700.00
Page 162
Basketweave and Floral Tea Set...... 425.00–525.00
Wardle Mustache Cup and Saucer 325.00–400.00
Wardle's Cup and Saucer 150.00–175.00
    Sugar Bowl................... 200.00–225.00
Page 163
Water Lily Teapot.................. 225.00–250.00
Water Lily Coffee Cup and Saucer 275.00–325.00
Wedgwood Teapot 600.00–700.00
Wild Rose and Trellis Tea Cup 150.00–175.00
Page 164
Bird In Flight and Pond Lily Vase 275.00–325.00
Bird On Tree Branch................ 175.00–200.00
Page 165
Classical Harp Vase 225.00–275.00
Etruscan Celery Vase 650.00–750.00
Footed Bird Vase 550.00–650.00
Page 166
G.J. Bird's Nest and Bird Vases.... 3,500.00–4,500.00
Geo. Jones Classical Putti Vases .. 1,500.00–2,000.00
G.J. Classical Putti w/Shells Vases.. 1,500.00–2,000.00
Page 167
Lilac Throated Song Bird Vases....... 325.00–375.00
Lion Footed Cobalt Vase 275.00–325.00
Pineapple Hand Vase 850.00–950.00
Page 168
Pineapple Hand Vase............... 275.00–325.00
Crane and Prunus Vase............. 275.00–325.00
Page 169
Songbird w/Triple Throated Vase.... 300.00–350.00
Triplet Handled Urn Group.......... 300.00–350.00
Thomas Shirley Ram Head Vase 275.00–325.00
Page 170
Boy and Girl Candlesticks........... 175.00–200.00
Wedgwood Figural Candlesticks.... 1,200.00–1,700.00

Worcester Dolphin Candlestick 475.00–600.00
Page 171
Boy Riding a Dolphin Centerpiece 550.00–650.00
Deer Head Cigarette Holder 200.00–225.00
Etruscan Shell/Seaweed Cuspidor... 1,200.00–1,700.00
Etruscan Sunflower Cuspidor..... 1,100.00–1,600.00
Page 172
Etruscan Sunflower Cuspidor....... 500.00–600.00
Fan Cuspidor 325.00–525.00
Floral Cuspidor.................... 325.00–525.00
Floral Cuspidor.................... 325.00–525.00
Page 173
Floral and Basketweave Cuspidor 325.00–525.00
Shell and Seaweed Cuspidor 375.00–575.00
Tenuous Majolica Shell Cuspidor ... 1,100.00–1,600.00
Page 174
Morning Glory Egg Basket w/Cups ... 500.00–600.00
Minton Twin Bird Inkwell 850.00–950.00
Page 175
Pond Lily Jardiniere 350.00–475.00
Wedgwood Blackberry Jardiniere...... 525.00–625.00
Wardle Bird and
    Fan Covered Matchbox.......... 350.00–450.00
Page 176
Elephant Match Holder 325.00–375.00
Drummer Boy Match Holder......... 325.00–575.00
Standing Monkey Match Holder 200.00–225.00
Floral and Fern Planter............ 325.00–400.00
G.J. Daisy and Banana Leaf Planter .. 1,100.00–1,300.00
Page 177
Geo. Jones Egyptian Style Planter .. 1,100.00–1,300.00
Minton Cattail Planter w/Underdish .. 600.00–800.00
Picket Fence and Raspberry Planter ... 375.00–475.00
Etruscan Salt and Pepper, pr... 1,100.00–1,600.00
Page 178
Wedgwood Salt Dip 425.00–525.00
Asparagus Server On Ocean Waves 300.00–325.00
Deer's Head Sweetmeat Server...... 300.00–350.00
G.J. Strawberry Server w/Spoon.... 1,300.00–1,600.00
Page 179
Geo. Jones Strawberry Server........ 700.00–800.00
Minton Asparagus Server 500.00–600.00
Rustic Handled Server 250.00–300.00
Strawberry Server with Individual Sugar Bowl and
    Cream Pitcher.................. 475.00–575.00
Page 180
Holdcroft Strawberry Serving Spoon ... 275.00–375.00
Unusual Floral Soap Dish 100.00–150.00
Page 181
Collection of Spoon Holders, var....... 125.00–225.00
Fan Spoon Holder.................. 150.00–175.00
Page 182
Chick Toothpick................... 250.00–275.00
Geo. Jones Trivet.................. 225.00–275.00
Etruscan Tumbler.................. 225.00–275.00
Page 183
Artist-Signed Umbrella Stand..... 6,000.00–7,000.00
T. Shirley Leopard Frog Handled Urn .. 375.00–475.00
Page 184
Geo. Jones Wine Caddy 6,000.00–7,000.00
Wedgwood Wine Cooler.......... 1,100.00–1,600.00
Boy Riding A Goat................ 700.00–900.00
Page 185
Conch Shell on Figural Coral 250.00–275.00
Geo. Jones Angels On Dolphins 1,100.00–1,600.00
Minton Boy and Girl With Shells 700.00–900.00
Minton Putti Carrying Shell 1,200.00–1,600.00

Schroeder's
ANTIQUES
Price Guide

. . . is the #1 best-selling antiques & collectibles value guide on the market today, and here's why . . .

• *More than 300 advisors, well-known dealers, and top-notch collectors work together with our editors to bring you accurate information regarding pricing and identification.*

• *More than 45,000 items in almost 500 categories are listed along with hundreds of sharp original photos that illustrate not only the rare and unusual, but the common, popular collectibles as well.*

• *Each large close-up shot shows important details clearly. Every subject is represented with histories and background information, a feature not found in any of our competitors' publications.*

• *Our editors keep abreast of newly developing trends, often adding several new categories a year as the need arises.*

If it merits the interest of today's collector, you'll find it in *Schroeder's.* And you can feel confident that the information we publish is up to date and accurate. Our advisors thoroughly check each category to spot inconsistencies, listings that may not be entirely reflective of market dealings, and lines too vague to be of merit. Only the best of the lot remains for publication.

Without doubt, you'll find
SCHROEDER'S ANTIQUES PRICE GUIDE
the only one to buy for
reliable information and values.

COLLECTOR BOOKS
A Division of Schroeder Publishing Co., Inc.